Proven
Garden
Tips

Proven
Garden
Tips from
Fine Gardening

The Taunton Press

Cover photo: Delilah Smittle
Copy/Production Editor: Diane Sinitsky
Layout Artist: Amy Bernard

Typeface: Berling
Paper: Glatfelter Writers Offset, 55 lb.
Printer: Bawden Printing, Eldridge, Iowa

Taunton

BOOKS & VIDEOS

for fellow enthusiasts

First Printing: 1996
Printed in the United States of America

The Taunton Press, 63 South Main Street, Box 5506,
Newtown, CT 06470-5506

Library of Congress Cataloging-in-Publication Data

Proven garden tips from Fine gardening.
        p. cm.
    Includes index.
        ISBN 1-56158-157-7 (alk. paper)
        1. Gardening. I. Fine gardening.
    SB453.P72 1996
    635.9–dc20   96-22443
                                             CIP

Contents

Introduction

Gardeners are inventive people. They like to come up with ways to use materials at hand to solve problems. In this book, you'll find a host of clever ideas for saving time and expense, from using pallets to make a quick compost bin to creating a slug trap from clay flower pots.

These tips, collected from the ever-popular tips column in *Fine Gardening* magazine, offer advice on how to grow healthy plants, both indoors and out. Since soil is the foundation of success, here are suggestions for improving it through mulching and composting. Getting plants off to a good start is the next step, and you'll also find a host of ideas for starting seeds, including easy-to-build hot beds and cold frames. Bulbs present their own set of challenges, so you'll find ideas for planting and protecting them. There are also pointers on plant care, covering fertilizing, training and pruning. In the section on watering, you'll find hints for making the best use of water in your garden. Since insects and animals are a vexation to nearly every gardener, here are many ecologically sound strategies for keeping them out. Because a garden is more than soil and plants, you'll find suggestions on how to attract birds. Finally, here are some ways to enjoy plants indoors. Whatever you grow, you'll find something in this book to make your thumb greener.

−Helen Albert, Associate Publisher
Gardening Books

Mulching & Composting

Saving kitchen scraps for the compost pile

I have come up with a routine that makes composting easier in these days of busy schedules. I accumulate kitchen scraps—vegetable peelings, tea bags, coffee grounds, bread crusts—in the plastic bags you get at the produce department of the supermarket. I keep a bag, closed tightly with a twist-tie, in the produce bin of the refrigerator, taking it out and adding to it when I am preparing vegetables or salads, or tossing out coffee grounds. The bag can stay in the refrigerator for at least a week without emitting foul odors. When the bag is full, I make one trip outside and dump the contents in my composter. I throw the bag out afterwards, but at least it has been reused once before going to the landfill.

–*Marge Giacalone, Port Washington, NY*

Discarded pallets make good compost bins

You can make a sturdy, easy-to-assemble compost bin from discarded pallets, the wooden platforms that allow forklifts to move packages. Stand four pallets on end and hold them together with tie wraps or wire, and your bin is ready for use (see the drawing below). The bin is just as easy to disassemble and move. Damaged pallets are often free for the taking from lumberyards. You may also find offers of free pallets in the want ads. Pallets aren't beautiful, but they're easy to paint if you want to improve their appearance.

–*Robert J. Wojcikowski, Poulsbo, WA*

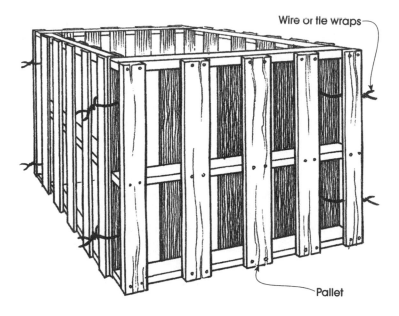

Wire or tie wraps

Pallet

Shredding leaves without a shredder

Here's an easy way to shred fallen leaves for the compost pile or next year's mulch. Put about two handfuls of leaves into a small garbage can. Then set an electric string trimmer on top of the leaves. Pull the trigger and move the trimmer up and down for several seconds. Stop and look at the leaves. If they're the size you want, continue to add leaves and shred them. If the leaves are bigger than you'd like, shred them some more. You'll soon get a feel for how long it takes to arrive at the texture you prefer.

–Robert E. Semrad, Hales Corners, WI

Large-scale composting

I garden on a wooded 4-acre lot. The soil is mostly sand and rock, and contains only the thinnest dusting of topsoil. For my 40th birthday, I asked for 4 yards of cow manure. I had not yet started composting and was desperate for organic matter. My gardens and I had a great season. However, well-rotted manure became difficult to obtain, so I became a dedicated composter. Turning the compost was a chore, and finding a place to put the stuff as I turned it was a challenge.

While visiting my sister, I discovered an ingenious solution, which has been successful for me for several years. The solution was to dedicate a 25-ft. by 25-ft. area of my property to composting. I drove rebar stakes into the ground and made a four-leaf-clover shape. I used four stakes per cloverleaf (see the drawing on the facing page) and hung chicken wire around the outside of the stakes. Each cloverleaf became a large bay for compost at various stages of decomposition. The center space is large enough for my wheelbarrow and me. The fencing keeps the compost contained in upright piles about 5 ft. deep, thus creating the critical mass necessary for nice hot composting.

The lower left bay is for new material. When the first bay is full, I stand in the center of the clover and move the organic matter from Bay 1 to Bay 2. By the time the compost reaches the last bay, it has been sufficiently turned. It takes six weeks for an apple core to move from Bay 1 to finished compost in Bay 4.

–Barbara Reitz, Sherborn, MA

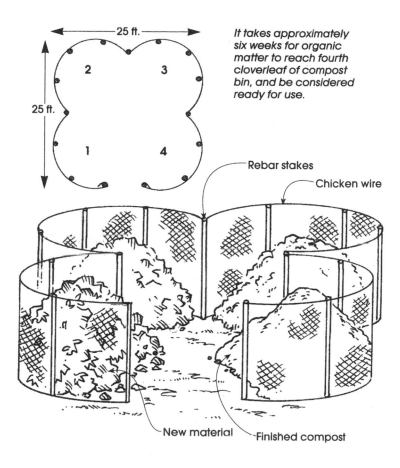

25 ft.

25 ft.

2   3

1   4

It takes approximately
six weeks for organic
matter to reach fourth
cloverleaf of compost
bin, and be considered
ready for use.

Rebar stakes

Chicken wire

New material   Finished compost

Jack-o'-lanterns guard compost pile

When Halloween is over, I put my carved pumpkins on the top board over my compost bin so I can enjoy the jack-o'-lanterns from the kitchen window. The squirrels feast on the pumpkin seeds scattered on the compost pile all through fall, and when the jack-o'-lanterns' faces cave in, I just toss the whole thing overboard into the compost bin.

–Patricia A. Owen, Newark, NY

Using large leaves to edge the compost pile

Weeds growing on the periphery of my compost pile are often a problem for me. I have been successful at keeping the weeds down by building up an "edge" of large leaves around the pile; it's best not to shred the leaves. I have found this substantially cuts down on the number of weeds that grow up along the outside of the compost pile. Eventually, the leaves break down on their own, leaving a weed-free pile of mulch. I use rhubarb leaves, but I suspect any large leaves would work as long as they don't take root.

—Ruth Fairall, Cordova, AK

Getting air to the center of a compost pile

When I began composting, one of the first things I learned was that oxygen is essential to the process of decomposition. So, to improve air circulation to the center of my compost piles, I built them

Build compost pile around cardboard construction tube, then remove tube to allow air circulation.

If you are adding material a bit at a time, use short section of tube to keep center free of debris and allow air to reach lower layers.

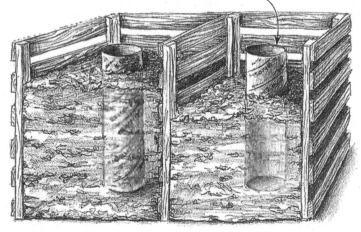

in the shape of a donut, with an open center. But as the piles grew taller, they became unstable and often collapsed into the hole.

My solution was to place a section of 6-in. to 8-in.-diameter construction tube (a cardboard cylinder used to make concrete footings) in the center of the compost bin. I build the piles around the tube, then remove it, leaving a large neat hole for air circulation (see the drawing on the facing page). I keep two sections of tube handy—one the height of the bin, the other only about 1 ft. long. If I'm adding a large amount of material, such as grass clippings or fallen leaves, or if I'm turning a pile, I use the longer tube. If I'm just adding a few spent flowers, I keep the short section in the top of the hole; the short tube prevents new material from falling into the hole while allowing air to reach the layers below.

Construction tube is inexpensive and available at most lumberyards. You can cut it easily with a razor blade, knife or saw. It lasts a season or two before breaking down.

–Roe A. Osborn, Wakefield, RI

Compost pit

On my tiny city lot, a compost heap would draw too much attention. So I tried pit composting. Now I have fresh compost each year, and as a bonus I grow crops in the pit.

My compost pits are really trenches, easy to hide behind tall plants. In spring, I dig a hole 1 ft. deep, 2 ft. wide and 4 ft. long for each pit. Some of the dirt goes on my planting beds, some to my impromptu trough gardens (planted in concrete blocks), and some stays beside the pit. Throughout the gardening season, I throw in any organic matter I can get my hands on, and top each layer with dirt from the nearby pile to discourage insects and adventurous pets. When I think of it, I splash on a pot of water from preparing vegetables or canning, and turn the layers. By the next spring, I have about a bushel of compost. Any material at the top of the pile that hasn't broken down completely goes into a new pit to act as a "starter."

One year, as I dug out finished compost, I realized that the pit was now fertile ground. On the spur of the moment, I planted some potatoes that had sprouted. I left 1 in. of compost in the pit, mixed it with 1 in. of soil and dropped in my sprouted potatoes. Then I covered them with more dirt, large tough-stemmed weeds and roughly torn newspaper, so that I could gather the crop by hand. To my delight, the harvest was excellent. I repeated the experiment the following year and got another bumper crop. Next year, I'll empty the pit, refill it with a mix of compost, soil, and sand or perlite, and sow carrots.

Compost pits are also a way to trick myself into expanding my planting area. I start new compost pits where I plan to expand my garden, and get the back-breaking work of digging out of the way a year or two before I plant.

—*Myra Mae McFarland, Fort Wayne, IN*

Newspaper eases change from lawn to border

Digging new garden beds in a lawn can be frustrating. Whether tilled or spaded, grass persists, and weeds such as dandelions seem imperishable. With newspaper and forethought, however, you can effortlessly subdue both turf and weeds before you turn the soil.

The secret is to starve the lawn to death by depriving plants of light. In late summer or fall, spread a layer of newspapers over the site of your future flower bed. Though just a few sheets of news-

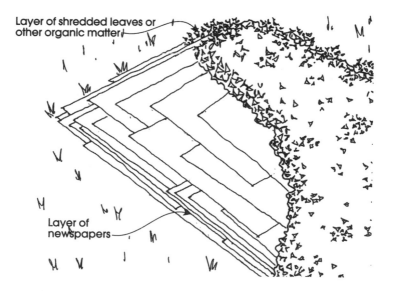

Layer of shredded leaves or other organic matter

Layer of newspapers

paper are sometimes enough, I usually put down a thickness of 20 to 40 sheets to ensure that the plants below are starved for light. Overlap the edges of the newspapers by an inch or more to eliminate gaps. To keep the newspapers from blowing away, cover them with 3 in. to 4 in. of hay, grass clippings, shredded leaves, bark or other organic matter (see the drawing on the facing page).

By the following spring, the site will be ready to be tilled or spaded. The dead roots of the grass and weeds, the pulpy newspaper and the top cover of organic matter will have become humus for your new garden. There is one drawback—you could find yourself sitting on the ground, absorbed in reading a news story you overlooked months ago!

—R.J. Siegler, Winthrop, ME

Double-duty composting

As a new gardener in a new home, I killed two flower plantings before realizing that I would have to improve my heavy clay soil. The clods I troweled around my plants turned into brickettes when they dried. I might as well have used wet cement.

After some reading, I decided to make compost and work it into my future flower beds. I made a small compost heap from leaves, grass clippings and ivy vine trimmings, interspersed with layers of cow manure. I hand-chopped everything to short lengths for rapid decomposition. I watered and turned the heap religiously, and within two weeks I had rich compost crawling with earthworms.

When I removed the compost, I discovered a bonus. The soil under the heap had loosened considerably, thanks to some very busy earthworms. Inspired, I made several small compost heaps on areas I planned to reseed with grass. When the compost was ready, I raked it out to a depth of several inches and sowed grass seed. The grass grew nicely. Where I once had barren ground, I now have a lawn. I've gone on to make compost heaps on problem spots in the flower beds and vegetable garden, with equally good results.

—Julia B. Dwyer, Cupertino, CA

Composting in buckets

Composting doesn't have to be a big production. I do a lot of my composting in the 5-gal. to 7-gal. plastic buckets that restaurants routinely throw away. These buckets are sturdy, and they come with a tight-fitting lid and a wire handle. To ready a bucket for composting, I drill nine ½-in. holes in the sides (three rows of three) and three in the bottom.

Composting is simple. I put 1 in. to 2 in. of soil in the bottom of a bucket and set it on the porch. My wife and I then add vegetable parings, fruit rinds and other organic kitchen waste until we accumulate a layer 3 in. or 4 in. thick (see the drawing below). I add another layer of soil, and we repeat the process, moistening the

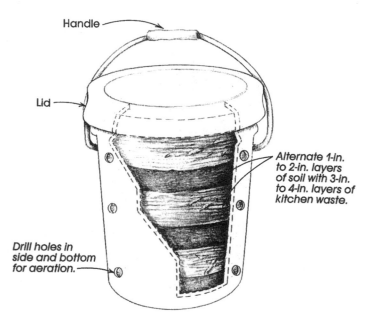

Handle

Lid

Alternate 1-in. to 2-in. layers of soil with 3-in. to 4-in. layers of kitchen waste.

Drill holes in side and bottom for aeration.

contents to keep them damp but not soggy. When the bucket is nearly full, we encourage decomposition by mixing everything together. I agitate the buckets often by rolling them around on the ground. You can also dump the contents out in a wheelbarrow and mix them with a spade, and return them to the bucket. When composting is complete, which usually takes two to six weeks in warm weather, I carry the humus to where I need it.

–*Charles Dawsey, Anacortes, WA*

Quick compost shredding

I have found an easy way to chop up garden waste for composting without a shredder.

I lay the waste on the empty ground near my compost heap in shallow piles 2 in. to 5 in. thick. I then chop sharply downward with a sharp spade until the pile is reduced to the size I want. I've become so quick at this that I can dispose of an average morning's clippings in a few minutes. I save my shredder for the brush pile.

If you don't have a sharp spade, I recommend you acquire one. It's useful for many things, including cutting through tree roots and opening bags of soil amendments. You can have your spade sharpened at a saw shop.

—Rachel Foster, Eugene, OR

Compost sifter

My husband and I use a lot of the compost we make as a mulch for our shrub beds. Because the compost sits on top of the ground rather than being incorporated into the soil, we like it to have a uniform, finely textured appearance. To filter out the larger, "unprocessed" chunks, we built two sifter boxes that allow us to screen two different sizes.

The boxes are simple rectangular frames made out of 2x4s screwed together at the corners. We sized them to fit squarely on top of our wheelbarrow. For sifting, we used two kinds of screens— hardware cloth for fine sifting, and two offset layers of 2-in.-sq. vinyl fencing for coarser sifting. We stretched the screens tightly and stapled them in place. A strip of lath along the outside of the box helps to secure the ends.

We sift the compost by lifting it, two scoops at a time, onto the screen with a pitchfork and then moving the compost back and forth across the mesh. The small particles fall into the wheelbarrow below. The large chunks that remain on the screen go back into the pile for further composting. When we first started sifting, we moved the compost around the screen with our hands. Then we discovered that using two 12-in. by 6-in. pieces of plywood makes the process go faster. Even with the fine mesh, we're able now to sift six wheelbarrows full in an hour. The finished product makes a lovely, healthy mulch for our beds.

–Mary Anne Cassin, Portland, OR

Patio composting

Half of my 10-ft. by 12-ft. patio garden is devoted to a patch of grass with ornamental and vegetable borders, and the other half is a concrete patio with plants in containers. Finding room for a functional yet sightly compost pile is challenging. My solution is a large plastic laundry hamper. Among its virtues are numerous perforations along the front and back panels that allow air circulation; a removable hinged lid that makes adding piecemeal vegetable matter such as kitchen scraps easy, but still keeps out the rain; and a scrubbable surface. And the hamper's neat, orderly appearance gives me the impression that I'm in control of my garden. I keep the hamper in the corner of the patio atop a small piece of plywood fitted with casters, and surround it with plants potted in containers of a matching color.

I'm a casual composter. Since my garden yields little organic matter, I collect leaves and grass clippings where I can, add plant trimmings and kitchen scraps, and alternate 6-in. layers of organic matter with a 1-in. layer of soil. When I leave the hamper alone for more than a year, I get fine-textured compost. Last year I emptied the hamper after four months. I got coarser, partially broken-down compost, which helped me start a new border and soon decomposed completely.

–Shanta Sundararajan, Richmond, BC, Canada

Mulch trees with moderation

I fear that lawnmowers and string trimmers may soon slip to number two on the infamous list of ways to kill trees. A lot of landscape contractors and gardeners injure and even kill trees by heaping mulch 6 in. and higher over the roots and right up to the trunk. Under the mulch, the trunk is constantly wet and in danger of invasion by decay organisms. Mice think the mulch is a first-rate nest, offering a hiding place with the tree's sugary inner bark and

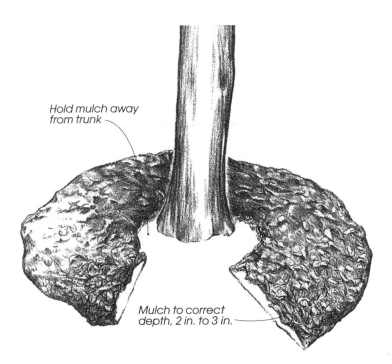

Hold mulch away
from trunk

Mulch to correct
depth, 2 in. to 3 in.

cambium on the doorstep. Small, newly transplanted trees often die because their little root systems are smothered.

Mulch is good for trees; it controls weeds, moderates soft temperatures and minimizes evaporation of soil moisture. But it need be no more than 2 in. to 3 in. deep (see the drawing above). Some landscapers say they reapply mulch to keep it looking fresh. To accomplish this, all you have to do is rake the surface of the mulch, or spread a thin layer of new mulch to replace what has decayed.

—Bonnie Lee Appleton, Virginia Beach, VA

Blending kitchen scraps for the compost pile

When I started adding kitchen scraps to my compost pile, the neighborhood squirrels, raccoons and possums were overjoyed. They took great pleasure in rooting through the pile and carrying off what they pleased.

Then I found a way to discourage the marauders. I pulverize the scraps in the blender before I add them to the pile. I keep the blender out on the counter and toss in vegetable and fruit peelings,

13

egg shells and other easily degradable bits of kitchen waste until the blender is full (which usually takes a day or two). Then I add a cup of water, push the puree button and pour the resulting mush on the compost heap. Blending these scraps has the added attraction of speeding up their decomposition.

—Sharon Spradlin-Barrett, Richmond, VA

Compost tumbler

I recently faced a common puzzle: how to make compost in a presentable way when the yard has no place to hide a compost pile. My husband came to the rescue. I was considering the compost bins and tumblers in garden catalogs, which look tidy but cost $100 and up, when he suggested I look instead for cylindrical garbage cans. I found exactly what I needed. Rubbermaid makes a 30-gal. model of heavy-gauge black plastic that rides on two wheels and has clamp handles to hold the lid on securely. I bought two (at $15 each) and drilled holes in the sides for aeration.

Composting with the garbage cans is easy. I fill them about half full (so they're not too heavy). I tip them over from time to time and roll them to mix the contents; the cylindrical shape and clamp-on lids make rolling possible. The black plastic absorbs the sun's heat, and the wheels let me trundle the cans around the yard. They're neat, inexpensive and portable—what more could I ask? If you try them, just be sure that your regular garbage cans are a different style or color, so family members won't dump the wrong household refuse in your compost.

—Janet P. Rushton, Warwick, RI

Tunnels for mulching rows of vegetables

Mulching vegetables controls weeds and conserves moisture, but applying the mulch can be a difficult operation. Seedlings are easily buried by the mulch; larger plants spread their foliage so that the mulch must be carefully tucked underneath, a slow and tedious process.

To make mulching vegetables grown in rows easier, I built tunnels out of 1x4 lumber to protect the plants while I mulch. Since I space my rows 1 ft. apart in beds 4 ft. wide, I built four tunnels, each 4 ft. to 5 ft. long. Using all four at once, I can mulch my beds in large sections.

Mulching with the help of the tunnels is a snap. I place the tunnels side by side over the rows of plants and then dump the mulch (I use sawdust or grass clippings) on top, smoothing and distributing it quickly with my hands. Then I slide the tunnels up the

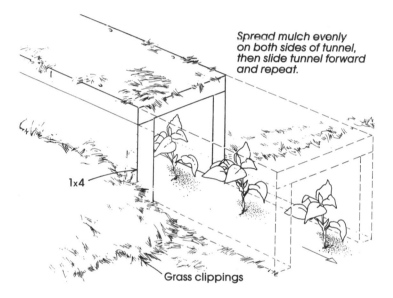

Spread mulch evenly on both sides of tunnel, then slide tunnel forward and repeat.

1x4

Grass clippings

rows and repeat the process (see the drawing above). There is little need for adjusting the mulch when I finish the rows.

Although each tunnel is only about 3½ in. high and 2 in. wide inside, it can be used to mulch taller and wider plants. The tunnel bends the plants over gently as I push it along the row; the plants pop back up again when the tunnel slides past.

–John Hillbrand, Bass, AR

A weed-free path

My mother-in-law gave me an idea for creating weed-free garden paths. For years she had thrown the leaves of her three large walnut trees into an adjoining meadow to avoid introducing their growth-inhibiting compound, juglone, into her garden. When we constructed additional raised beds last year, I used the walnuts' growth-inhibiting properties to our advantage.

By first placing layers of newspaper in the pathways, then adding walnut leaves, we have achieved weed-free pathways without affecting the plants within the raised beds. We add more every autumn as the decomposing leaves subside.

As winter progresses and we shell the walnuts, the cracked shells are scattered on top of the leaves, giving a clean, crunchy surface, which is a pleasure to walk on—even during the winter rains.

—Jessie Balding, Gold Hill, OR

Acorn mulch

Each autumn I accumulate a great quantity of leaves and acorns from the numerous oak trees on my property. I can't even rely on the squirrels to help get rid of acorns—with so may oak trees in the nearby woods, they seldom bother with mine. My solution is to turn the acorns into mulch. Chopped up in my small electric chipper-shredder, they make an attractive amendment to the flowers in my garden.

The acorn mulch can be laid on garden beds in the fall, but I prefer to store the whole acorns over winter and run them through the chipper-shredder in the early spring. I store them in plastic barrels in my basement. To prevent attracting rodents, I make sure the acorns are dry and covered securely. In spring the freshly chopped acorns make a handsome mulch around the blooming daffodils and emerging daylilies.

—Sandra Kocher, Spencer, MA

A mixed mulch

I garden in sandy soil and invest a lot of effort in trying to retain soil moisture during the summer. I have access to horse manure and wood shavings and to grass clippings. Either mulch used alone seems to create a barrier that prevents water from soaking through to the soil. But mixed together, they tend to compost in place and keep the soil moist even in the hottest weather. I have used this mixed mulch on fruit trees and grapes, and I'm starting to use it on dahlias. It may not be attractive enough for a flower bed, but it weathers quickly to an acceptable appearance.

–Stephen M. Ekstrand, Woodinville, WA

Cheesecloth mulch for lawns

In my landscaping business, I often use hay as a mulch when I install new lawns or reseed large areas. But for smaller jobs, I find that using cheesecloth is much more practical than lugging around a heavy bale of hay for a few handfuls of mulch.

Cheesecloth is lightweight and easy to store. It also stops birds from eating the grass seed; contains no weed seeds, as hay often does; and looks neat. The new grass quickly grows through the cloth, hiding it from view. There's no need to take the cloth up because it rots within a year or so—along with the bamboo pegs, cut from standard green stakes, that I use to hold the cloth in place. You can buy small quantities of cheesecloth from grocery stores. Fabric stores sell it by the yard.

–Thomas A. Vasale, Charleston, WV

Propagation

Separating seeds from chaff

I have an easy way of separating the chaff from the seeds I collect in my garden. In a shallow, rectangular pan or the lid to a box of stationery (something with a light-colored lid makes it easier to distinguish seeds from chaff), I liberate the seeds and remove large pieces of debris with my fingers. Then I tilt the pan or lid away from me to send seeds and the remaining debris into a far corner. Next, I slowly tilt the pan until the seeds start to roll. If the chaff tries to catch up with the seeds, I push it away with an index card. I keep collecting chaff with the card until most of the seeds have rolled free. Then I scoop out the chaff with the card and pour the seeds into an envelope for storage.

—*Mary Ann McGourty, Norfolk, CT*

Reflectors keep light on plants

My wife and I have tinkered with the fluorescent fixtures that we use for seed-starting to get more light on our seeds. To catch light that would otherwise scatter uselessly into the surrounding dark-

18

ness, we made reflectors from the heavy, foil-covered paper once commonly used in house construction (heavy-duty aluminum foil from the grocery store would also work). Seedlings along the edges of our flats lean less toward the fluorescent tubes than seedlings grown without reflectors. We believe that the reflectors also keep the humidity around the plants somewhat higher than that of the surrounding air. As the drawing below shows, a strip of reflecting paper between two fixtures allows us to grow healthy seedlings in three 11-in.-wide trays instead of just two.

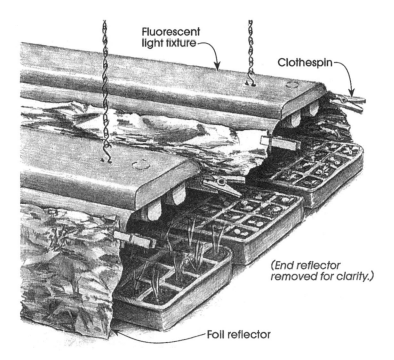

Fluorescent light fixture

Clothespin

(End reflector removed for clarity.)

Foil reflector

The only tool you need is a pair of scissors. We cut five reflectors—one to hang between our two light fixtures (which are about 12 in. apart), two to drape from the outer edges of the fixtures around the trays of plants and two to enclose the ends. We attach the reflectors to the fixtures with clothespins—two per reflector. You could use tape instead, but we find that clothespins make it easier to remove the reflectors when it's time to water the plants.

—*Perry L. Willis, Southampton, NJ*

Inexpensive homemade light box

After years of trying to start plants from seed in a house lacking a spot that is both warm and well lit, I decided to construct my own light box. I built the box out of readily available materials: a 4-ft. by 8-ft. panel of rigid ¾-in. foil-covered insulation, a 2x4, duct tape, 16d finishing nails, a 4-ft. fluorescent light fixture and long wood screws. I sized the box to hold five 10-in. by 18-in. growers' trays fitted with clear plastic lids, with room left over for a few pots. If your trays have different dimensions, alter the design accordingly.

I cut the insulation panel to a 6-ft. length, then cut that piece into three 16-in.-wide sections using a sharp knife held at a 45° angle to create a beveled edge (see the drawing below). When mak-

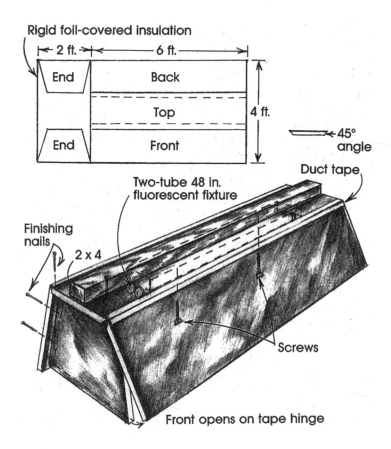

Rigid foil-covered insulation

2 ft. — 6 ft.

End   Back

Top   4 ft.

45° angle

End   Front

Two-tube 48 in. fluorescent fixture

Duct tape

Finishing nails

2 x 4

Screws

Front opens on tape hinge

ing the beveled cuts, be sure that the angles of both cuts point to the center of the panel. Using duct tape for a flexible hinge, I put the pieces together to form a bottomless box. To cut the ends, I stood the box on end on the remaining 2-ft. length of insulation, scored a line along the inside of the box as a cutting guide, then repeated the process for the other end. Then I cut the ends and attached them to the top and back with finishing nails. I attached the light fixture to the inside of the top section with screws long enough to pass through the insulation board and bite into a 2x4 running lengthwise on top of the insulation board. The lights are controlled by a timer.

The box works well for starting many seeds. The foil reflects light all around the new seedlings, and the heat from the light tubes keeps the inside temperature 85°F to 90°F. In the box, most seeds germinate in half the time they require under less ideal conditions. Seedlings usually can be moved out of the light box after three or four weeks.

—*Janice Hocking, Raleigh, NC*

5¢ greenhouses

I've found an inexpensive alternative to the widely sold miniature greenhouses that improve seed germination by providing light and even moisture. I covet the mini-greenhouses—clear plastic domes for flowerpots, flats with clear lids—but balk at their prices. I get the same benefits by modifying recyclable 2-liter plastic soda bottles, which cost 5¢ in those enlightened states where a bottle deposit is required.

I use soda bottles that are made in two pieces, a transparent body that fits into an opaque, flat-bottomed holder. I dip the bottom in very hot (but not boiling) water to soften the dabs of glue that hold the pieces together, and then I pry them apart. Next I temporarily reassemble the pieces, draw a line around the clear body where they meet, pull them apart, cut ½ in. below the line, and discard the bottom piece of the clear body. After I rinse the clear top and opaque bottom in a mild solution of chlorine bleach, they're ready for use.

I punch a few extra holes in the bottom piece for drainage (some are there already), and add moistened potting mix. The bottom is about 4½ in. in diameter and 2½ in. deep—ideal for a modest number of seeds. The top piece fits snugly inside the bottom, completing the greenhouse, and you can remove and replace the screw cap to control ventilation. You can also use the top piece alone to cover a flowerpot. If you pick the right pot, the top makes a good tight fit inside the rim.

–*Sydney Eddison, Newtown, CT*

Miniature greenhouse for propagating plants

I've made a miniature greenhouse by cutting and assembling polystyrene panels into a 24-in. by 13⅝-in. rectangular box. My greenhouse is ideal for growing seedlings and cuttings under fluorescent lights.

Most hardware stores sell packages of six polystyrene panels for about $4. The panels are ¾ in. by 13⅝ in. by 48 in. Other materials needed are: all-purpose white glue, four 1¼-in. wire nails

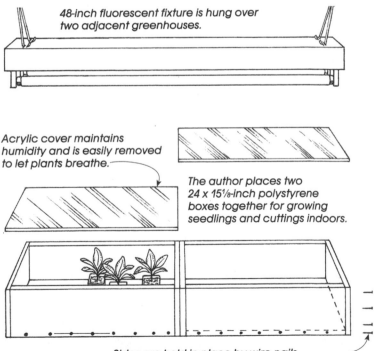

48-inch fluorescent fixture is hung over two adjacent greenhouses.

Acrylic cover maintains humidity and is easily removed to let plants breathe.

The author places two 24 x 15⅛-inch polystyrene boxes together for growing seedlings and cuttings indoors.

Sides are held in place by wire nails.

and a sheet of clear acrylic plastic. I cut the panels with a sharp knife to the following dimensions: one bottom piece, 24 in. by 13⅝ in.; two small side pieces, 6¾ in. by 15⅛ in.; two large side pieces, 6¾ in. by 24 in. I assembled the pieces into a rectangular box (see the drawing on the facing page) and temporarily held them in place with the wire nails to check the fit. Then I removed the nails from the side pieces and glued the sides together. Various glues may work, but I found plain white glue satisfactory.

After applying glue to all the contact points, I put the nails back in. When the glue dried, I applied caulking compound to all the joints, making the box leakproof. Then I used a piece of clear acrylic plastic as a cover.

These panels make a greenhouse big enough to hold one standard 11x21-in. plastic seedling tray or two 11-in.-sq. bays. My light source was a 48-in. fluorescent light hung over two adjacent boxes.

The cover keeps in the humidity, although I remove it occasionally so the seedlings can breathe. When it's time to harden off the plants, I simply pick up my box and bring it outside.

—*Jonas L. Bassen, Bowie, MD*

Trees in flats

We start trees from seeds in homemade containers that produce well-branched root systems ready for transplanting. In an ordinary nursery pot, the primary root of a seedling tree soon hits bottom, starts circling and branches into a matted snarl. At transplanting, you have two unwelcome choices: Cut off the snarl, which sets the tree back, or leave the snarl and risk having roots strangle each other. In our containers, when any root reaches the bottom, it stops elongating and branches—no snarl.

The container is basically a deep, open-bottomed flat, with one special feature—we staple copper window screen across the bottom. Copper inhibits the elongation of root tips. The screen also air-prunes roots that grow through it. When a root reaches bottom in one of our flats, it stops and branches. Soon the young trees have well-branched root systems. We nail three 1x1 runners to the bottom of the flat so air can circulate under the screen. We make 20-in.-sq. flats of 1x6 lumber, which gives us enough depth for 5 in. of soil mix and no more weight than we can carry comfortably. We can grow seedlings very close together or widely spaced. When the roots need more room, we move the plants to containers. Slow growers may stay in flats for a year or more.

—Bill Nelson, Pacific Tree Farms, Chula Vista, CA

A light box for starting seeds

I've come up with an apparatus that provides both light and warmth for the seedlings I start in my basement. The apparatus is nothing more than a box made of foil-covered insulation board. The top of the box rests on light fixtures that hang from the joists that support the floor above. When I raise or lower the lights to keep them in proximity to the plants, the top of the box moves with the fixtures; the bottom remains stationary on a table.

Assembling a light box like mine is easy. You'll need a table to support the box and several items you can find at a lumberyard or a home-center store; one or more fluorescent shop-light fixtures;

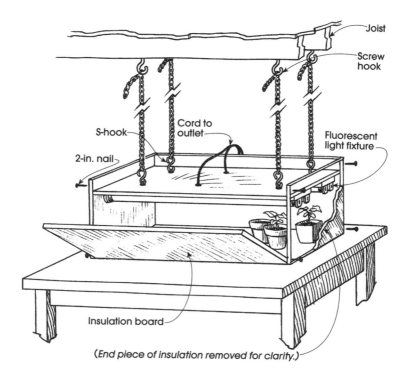

(End piece of insulation removed for clarity.)

#16 single steel jack chains, S-hooks and screw hooks to hang the lights; 1-in.-thick, foil-covered insulation board (other thicknesses are also available); and at least eight 2-in.-long nails. Begin by positioning the table under the joists; it's easiest to have the long sides of the table run parallel to the joists (see the drawing on the facing page). Then drill holes into the joists for the screw hooks—two per light fixture—and screw them into place. With bolt cutters or heavy-duty wire cutters, cut the chain to lengths equal to the distance from the joists to the lowest position of the light fixtures.

Next, assemble the box. With a utility knife, cut two pieces of insulation board for the bottom and top. Poke holes through the top piece, and thread the chains through the holes. Attach the light fixtures to the chains with S-hooks so the top board rests on the fixtures. Then hang the light assembly from the screw hooks.

The last step is to cut four more pieces of insulation board for the sides of the box. The height of the sides will depend on how high you anticipate raising the lights. I sometimes put houseplants under my lights, so the sides of my box are about 2½ ft. tall. If you use your light box only to start seeds, 18 in. should be plenty. Attach the sides to each other and to the bottom of the box with nails. Leave the heads of the nails protruding slightly so that you can remove them with ease.

I've been using my light box for three years now with great success. The reflective coating on the insulation board bounces light around so that the plants get more light emitted by the fixtures, and the insulating properties of the board trap heat generated by the lights, eliminating the need for bottom heat even in a cool basement. The sides of the box are easy to pull apart to gain access to the plants for watering. Although I open the box as often as once a day, the nails continue to hold well.

—Diane Elliott, Sewickley, PA

A hoop-house cold frame

Here is a simple design for a cold frame that helps me get a jump on the growing season. My cold frame isn't the traditional wooden box covered with an old window sash; it looks more like the

Quonset-hut-shaped hoop houses that nurseries often use to over-winter tender plants or plants in containers. The frame is made of flexible ½-in. and ¾-in. PVC pipes. The covering is heavy, clear, 4-mil or 6-mil plastic sheeting attached to the frame with duct tape or clear plastic packing tape. My hoop-house cold frame is quite large—about 4 ft. wide and more than 8 ft. long—but you can modify my basic design to suit your needs.

A hoop house like mine is easy to build—and just as easy to dis-assemble for storage. From a hardware store or a lumberyard, pur-

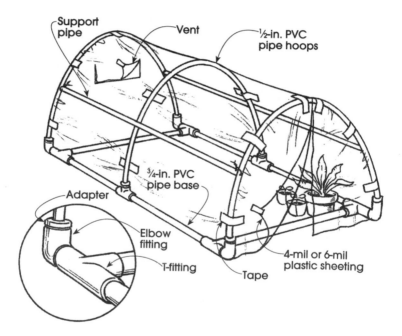

chase clear plastic sheeting, PVC pipe (I used ¾-in. pipe for the base of the frame and ½-in. pipe for the hoops and supports) and three kinds of PVC fittings—elbows, T's and ¾-in.-to-½-in. adapters. You'll also need a small amount of PVC glue. Begin by putting together the long sides of the base. Decide on the number of central hoops you want—I used one for an 8-ft.-long hoop house—and with a hacksaw cut lengths of PVC to fit between the hoops. Glue a length of PVC into either end of a T-fitting and glue a combination T-fitting and elbow fitting to round the corner at the ends (see detail in drawing above). Then cut the end pieces and the hoops to the desired length and insert them into the fittings with the aid of $^3/_4$-in.-to-$^1/_2$-in. adapters. Don't use glue here if you want to be able to pull the frame apart for storage.

Next, if your frame needs extra support, cut support pipes the length of the hoop house, attaching them to the hoops with pieces of wire drawn through holes drilled in the PVC. Finally, cover the frame with plastic—one large sheet over the top and a half-circle for each end. Attach the plastic to itself and to the frame with tape, and your hoop house is ready for use. The house is very light, so use tent stakes to secure the frame to the ground or weight it down with bricks to prevent a strong wind from carrying it away.

I use my hoop-house cold frame to extend my seed-starting space. As quarters get tight indoors, I move the larger seedlings into the cold frame. On sunny days, when temperatures inside the frame can rise to dangerous levels even though outdoor temperatures are cool, I vent the frame by taping open vents I cut in each end, making sure to close them again at the end of the day. When it's warm enough to set plants outdoors without protection, I fold up the plastic sheeting and pull apart the frame and store it until the following spring. You could also cover the frame with shade cloth to protect sensitive plants from hot summer sun and cover the frame again with plastic in the fall to extend the season for vegetables and tender container plants.

—*Janet Tracy, Kansas City, MO*

No-backache cold frame

Several years ago I built a cold frame as a protected environment to harden off seedlings in the spring and to propagate perennials and shrubs from cuttings in the summer. The cold frame served me well until I developed back problems, which have made stooping down to reach into a ground-level frame painful. I didn't want to stop using this valuable garden tool, so I designed a small storage cabinet with a cold frame on top so I could work with my plants while standing up.

The construction of the cabinet required nothing more than basic carpentry skills. I used 1x3, 2x3 and 2x4 pine (including pressure-treated pieces for the base) to build a frame, then sheathed the frame with $^1/_4$-in. plywood. The resulting cabinet is

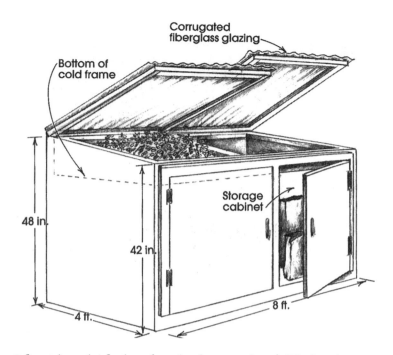

Corrugated
fiberglass glazing

Bottom of
cold frame

Storage
cabinet

48 in.

42 in.

4 ft.

8 ft.

8 ft. wide and 4 ft. deep (see the drawing above). The height at the front is 42 in., a little more than waist high for a person of average height. The back of the frame is 6 in. taller; the sloping lid allows the corrugated fiberglass glazing to collect more sunlight and allows rain to run off. In my design, the bottom of the cold frame sits on a shelf that is recessed 6 in. into the cabinet, so that the cold frame can accommodate plants up to 12 in. high at the back.

I appreciate the extra storage space in the cabinet for tools and bags of peat moss and perlite, but the real benefit of my cold frame design is no more backaches!

–Jonas L. Bassen, Bowie, MD

More uses for row covers

I've found several alternative uses for row covers, those wispy fabrics and films that generally are used to provide frost protection in spring and fall.

I sow the seeds of tender plants like corn under row covers. Germination is quicker, the seedlings thrive until they outgrow their cover, and harvest comes a week early.

Row covers start to break up after two to three years of exposure, but I save the pieces to shelter small transplants during their first week in the garden. I set a bamboo stake close to the transplant and drape the piece of row cover over it. I lay even smaller pieces of old row cover atop newly sown seeds to hasten germination.

I grow some crops under row covers from sowing to harvest to protect them from insects. I get onions and radishes with no root-maggot damage at all by growing the plants in row-cover tunnels supported by hoops of wire or PVC pipe.

Strawberries often winter-kill here, even when mulched, but my bed comes through in good shape under a row cover. I like to hold down the row cover with hairpin-shaped anchors, 1 in. wide and 6 in. long, made from coat hangers or wire of similar gauge. I bunch up a bit of fabric every 3 ft. along the edge, making little "ears," and push an anchor over each ear—a stronger arrangement than poking anchors through the row cover would be.

–Molly Hackett, Victor, MT

Seed sifting

After harvesting the seed heads from my chives, I wondered how I could separate the tiny black seeds from the chaff. I found the perfect tool in my kitchen: the flour sifter. It's the type with a side crank and rotary wires inside. I separated the dried flowers from the stalk, dropped them in and cranked away. The seeds fell through the screen and the chaff stayed behind. I'm sure this technique will work for other flowers with small seeds.

–Roxie Powell, Longmont, CO

Chamomile tea for seedlings

An effective way I have found to control damping-off of seedlings is to use chamomile tea. I use one chamomile tea bag in 4 cups of boiling water, and allow it to sit for 24 hours to ensure that I have a strong brew at room temperature. I pour the tea into a plant mister and spray the seedlings as soon as they appear, and each time I water them. I continue this until the seedlings have developed their second set of leaves.

–Jesse Vernon Trail, Vernon, BC, Canada

Homemade hot bed

For about $20, I made a flat for starting tender plants from seeds. It's insulated and heated from the bottom, and it produced good germination and growth in a cold greenhouse in January.

I made the flat with heating cable and rigid foil-faced foam insulation (see the drawing below). The insulation is available in 4-ft. by 8-ft. sheets at almost any building-supply store, and cuts easily with a sharp knife. Many mail-order suppliers sell bottom-heating cables, as well as bottom-heating mats and tapes.

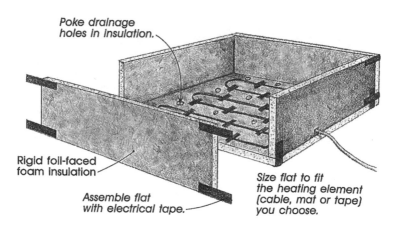

Poke drainage holes in insulation.

Rigid foil-faced foam insulation

Assemble flat with electrical tape.

Size flat to fit the heating element (cable, mat or tape) you choose.

For the bottom of the flat, I cut out a rectangular piece of insulation. You can vary the shape and dimensions of the bottom to suit your needs and to accommodate almost any soil heater. I laid out the heating cable in runs 2 in. apart, fastened them with electrical tape, and poked drainage holes in the insulation. Then I cut sides 6 in. tall, assembled them with electrical tape, and filled the flat 3 in. to 4 in. deep with potting soil. The flat won't hold up if you move it around, but mine worked fine for six months on a greenhouse bench.

—Jennifer Sanders, Orcas, WA

Easy cold treatment for seeds

My wife tolerates flats of seedlings in front of every window we have, but she will not tolerate a refrigerator full of seeds, so I can't follow the usual recommendation to put seeds in a plastic bag with damp peat moss and store them in the refrigerator. So how do I start my seeds? I put our long, midwestern winters to use.

I sow my seeds directly in cell packs in a moist potting mix, set the cell packs in flats, put the flats in a plastic bag, and set everything on a shelf in my unheated garage, where the conditions are cold but never much below freezing. Once the seeds have received the recommended period of chilling, I bring them indoors and set them under lights for germination. Sowing directly in cell packs saves a great deal of time—I handle the seeds only once.

—*Tom Micheletti, Barrington, IL*

A seedling shuttle

I start lots of seeds indoors, but I don't have adequate light to allow all my seedlings to grow as vigorously as they might. So as soon as they are up, I start taking them outdoors on sunny, warm days, and I bring them back in at night for warmth. I used to make several trips in and out every morning and every evening, carrying the flats one by one. Then I saw a lightweight, rolling television stand at the Salvation Army store for $6. The stand holds four trays on its two shelves. Now, instead of eight trips in and out each day, I make only two. The stand is light enough to lift over a threshold or to carry up and down a few steps.

—*Susan Scott Witt, Potter Valley, CA*

Sterilize soil in the pressure cooker

Sterilized soil is often recommended as a growing medium for cuttings, but preparing it is often easier said than done. I found a way to do the job easily without the smell and mess. I scoop the soil into tin cans with covers (butter-cookie tins are ideal), and place the cans in a pressure cooker. I add about ½ in. water and cook at 15 pounds for 15 minutes, then let everything cool. The steam permeates and sterilizes the soil without changing its texture, and there's no messy cleanup.

—*Ted Knapp, Minooka, IL*

A painless way to separate rooted cuttings

I propagate many plants by rooting cuttings in a potting mix. I usually have five or six going at a time in the same container. Frequently, the roots of the cuttings fill the potting mix, making it difficult to separate them at planting time. I've found that if I shake free the excess soil and then place the cuttings into a bowl of water, most of the tangled roots float apart. Those roots that remain tangled can be pulled free with very little damage.

—Linda Young, Broken Arrow, OK

Germinating hard-shelled seeds

I used to have a hard time getting okra seeds to germinate. I tried soaking them in water, but without luck. Then a friend suggested I try freezing them. It worked like a charm. Now I put two or three seeds in each section of an ice cube tray, cover them with water and slide the tray into the freezer. A day or so later I plant the ice cubes. Every seed germinates. I haven't tried yet, but I bet this technique will work with all sorts of seeds that are slow to take up water, such as sweet peas, four o'clocks and morning-glories.

—Carolyn Hallman, Rock Hill, SC

Support for lightweight seed cups

If you've ever started plants from seeds in polystyrene or paper cups, you know how unstable these cups can be, especially when they contain relatively large seedlings. I've devised the following plywood tray that gives seed cups extra support.

The tray was easy to make. The cups I use are 3 in. in diameter, so to give future seedlings enough space, I cut a piece of ½-in. plywood to a multiple of 4 in. in both length and width. I based my ultimate dimensions (24 in. by 16 in.) on what would fit conveniently in our window greenhouse. Next, I measured in 4 in. from two adjoining sides and marked the center for a corner hole. From this point I measured all the other hole centers on a 4-in. grid. With a jigsaw (a holesaw or flycutter will also do the job), I cut holes ¼ in. smaller in diameter than the tops of the cups. Then I

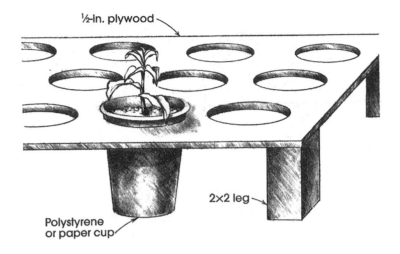

½-In. plywood

2x2 leg

Polystyrene
or paper cup

cut four legs of equal length out of 2x2 lumber so that the bottoms of the cups would be suspended ¼ in. above the surface the tray sits on (see the drawing above). I attached the legs to the plywood and the job was done.

My seed-cup tray works beautifully. I no longer have to worry about knocking the seedlings over. And carrying the cups around in the tray is a lot quicker and easier than dealing with single cups.

–Roe A. Osborn, Wakefield, RI

Starting seeds in measuring cups

The small plastic measuring cups that come in boxes of laundry detergent make great pots for starting seeds. After rinsing out residual detergent that may cling to the cups, poke drainage holes in the bottoms with an ice pick or a hammer and nail. To conserve space, cut the handles off with a pair of scissors or tin snips. Label your seeds by writing their names directly on the sides of the cups with a felt-tip marker.

–Eddie M. Zanrosso, Pasadena, CA

Germinating seeds in petri dishes

To germinate small seeds that need extra care, I use petri dishes—round, shallow, lab containers. First, I line the dishes with paper circles cut from cone-shaped coffee filters. Then I moisten the filter paper, sprinkle on the seeds, add the lids and store the dishes in a safe spot until the seeds germinate (see the drawing below). For seeds that require a period of chilling to germinate, I first put the dishes in the vegetable drawer of my refrigerator.

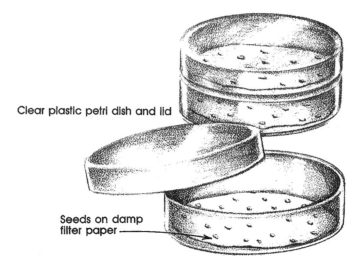

Clear plastic petri dish and lid

Seeds on damp filter paper

I think petri dishes have a lot of advantages. The dishes, which are roughly 4 in. in diameter and ½ in. high, are stackable, so I can store a lot of them in a small space. I prefer them to plastic bags because they're easier to handle. Finally, they're made of clear plastic, so I can easily check the seeds.

Be sure to use good-quality coffee-filter paper. I've found that paper towels work well for seeds that germinate rapidly, but are trouble for seeds that have to be chilled or seeds that germinate slowly. Some name-brand paper towels contain a germicide that can inhibit seed germination. Generic paper towels have no germicide, but they can develop molds within a few weeks.

My petri dishes are relatively inexpensive—about $16 per hundred. I bought them through a laboratory supply catalog.

—*Karen Jescavage-Bernard, Croton-on-Hudson, NY*

Using PVC pipe for starting seeds

For starting seeds of black walnuts, hickories, oaks and other trees that have deep taproots, I make long containers from 18-in. to 24-in. lengths of 4-in.-diameter PVC pipe, with hardware cloth pushed in one end to contain the potting soil (see the drawing below). There are similar commercial containers available abroad,

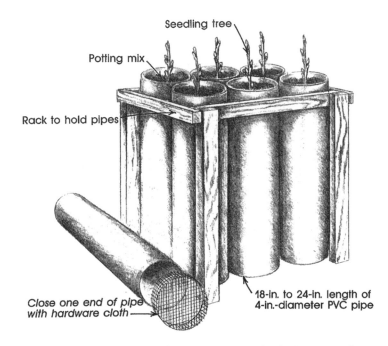

Seedling tree

Potting mix

Rack to hold pipes

Close one end of pipe with hardware cloth

18-in. to 24-in. length of 4-in.-diameter PVC pipe

but I have not found any of them here. While the homemade containers have several disadvantages—cost, awkward handling and an inclination to tip unless held in a frame—they allow seedling trees to develop deep roots that remain intact during transplanting. Moisten the potting mix to remove the young tree.

—Karen Jescavage-Bernard, Croton-on-Hudson, NY

Corsage boxes for germination

Searching for something in which to start some geranium seeds, I came across an old, clear plastic corsage box. I poked drainage holes in the bottom half, added damp starter-soil mix, sowed about 50 seeds, closed the cover—and voilà! a mini greenhouse. The seeds germinated in record time, and the box was large enough to hold the seedlings until they were ready for transplanting into individual pots. (Please note that I reopened the box and left it open once the seeds germinated.) If you don't have a corsage box, you can use the plastic boxes that strawberries are sometimes packaged in or containers from salad bars.

–*Ruby Thomas, Anacortes, WA*

Germinating seeds in egg shells

Believe it or not, you can start seeds in egg shells. After using large eggs, rinse and save the shell halves in their cartons. When you

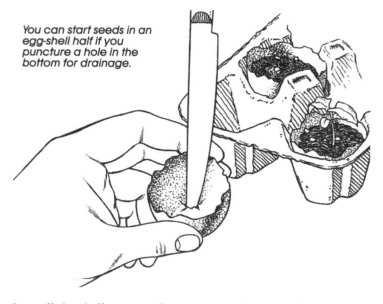

You can start seeds in an egg-shell half if you puncture a hole in the bottom for drainage.

have all the shells you need, puncture the bottom of each one with a sharp knife for drainage (see the drawing above). Then put the shells back into the carton and fill them with moistened growing mix. Sow one seed in each shell half. When the seedlings are ready for planting, crush the shell gently or remove it as you set the seedling into the ground.

–*Gretchen L. Proos, Richland, MI*

Empty toilet-paper rolls as seed starters

I save empty toilet-paper rolls all year to make seed-starting pots in late winter or early spring. I cut the rolls in half, fill them with soilless mix by scooping them through a tub of pre-moistened mix, sow seeds (one per roll) and set the rolls, sides touching, in a pan. I water by filling the pan, pouring off the excess water after the mix becomes saturated. The rolls often grow mold on their sides, but the mold doesn't seem to bother seedlings; I've never had a problem with damping off, a fungus that topples seedlings.

Like peat pots, toilet-paper rolls can wick moisture away from newly planted seedlings, causing them to dry out even when they are in moist ground. So when planting out seedlings, bury the edges of the rolls below the surface of the soil, or peel the rolls away from the rootballs.

—Agnes deBethune, Jersey City, NJ

Starting seeds in limited space

Years ago, when I first began starting large numbers of plants from seeds, I had half the space I really needed. I squeezed lights and seed trays in the basement of my small house, and often lacked room to set things down. I reached my limit the day I accidentally knocked over several flats and lost a lot of sedum seedlings that I wouldn't be able to replace until the next winter.

I looked for a space-saving alternative to starting seeds in flats, and found it in an article on testing grass seeds for viability by using moist paper toweling in a plastic bag. I adopted the method for my ornamental seeds, and have been pleased with the results ever since.

I spread out a sheet of moistened paper towel, sprinkle seeds on one half, and fold the other half over them. Since I generally use zip-closing sandwich bags, I fold the towels once more to fit neatly inside the bags. Even with two folds, I can easily check for germination by holding the bags up to the light. I seal the bags tightly and use a marking pen to label them with the genus and species, estimated germination time, and present date. If the seeds need cold stratification, I put the bags in the refrigerator. Otherwise, I put the bags in a heated room out of direct sunlight.

As seeds sprout, I transplant them to cell-packs. I'm careful not to break the new roots. If a seed sticks to the towel, I rewet the paper or rip off a piece with the seed.

On balance, I like starting with paper towels. Transplanting is no more tedious than thinning a flat of overcrowded seedlings. I sometimes see mold on seeds that have been moist for several months, but it doesn't seem to affect germination, and if it gets too severe, I just change the paper. The bags save lots of room, and they let me pick out only the seeds I need or have space for at the time. If I'm in a real pinch for room, I just let some bags stratify longer in the refrigerator.

—Suzette Visentin, Niagara Falls, ON, Canada

Strawberry containers as seedling covers

I've discovered that plastic-mesh strawberry containers make handy shade covers for newly transplanted seedlings. After planting and watering, I cover each plant with a container, which I leave in place for several days until the plant becomes acclimated to life outdoors. If the weather is dry, I can water covered seedlings right through the strawberry container. The containers last indefinitely, are easy to stack for storage, and come in pint and quart sizes.

—Wally Kalbfleisch, Warrenton, VA

Seedling transplant protection

With a little modification, a ½-gal. paper milk carton can protect seedlings that are newly set outdoors from sun, wind and frost until the plants have become acclimated to their environment.

I start by opening the top of the carton completely. With scissors, I cut down each corner to the shoulder of the carton to form four rectangular flaps. Then I turn the carton over and cut the bottom from corner to corner, following the "X" to form four triangular flaps (see the drawing on the facing page), and the carton is ready for use as a plant protector.

To protect a young transplant from sun and wind, open the four top flaps and lower the carton, top end first, over the plant. Mound some soil on each flap to hold the carton in place. If a late frost threatens, simply push down the triangle-shaped flaps to

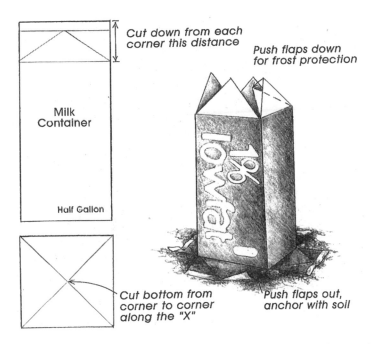

Cut down from each corner this distance

Push flaps down for frost protection

Milk Container

Half Gallon

Cut bottom from corner to corner along the "X"

Push flaps out, anchor with soil

close the carton and hold them in place with a small flat rock. Reopen the carton the next morning after the danger of frost has passed.

When the plants no longer need protection (I find that a week or ten days is usually enough), remove the carton and flatten it for storage. I wrap one or two dozen cartons together with masking tape. This way I can quickly count how many I have on hand. With a little care, these cartons last for several seasons.

–Kirby F. Neubert, Cabot, PA

Inexpensive homemade hot bed

I've discovered that the foam crates used to ship grapes to market make good homemade hot beds. The crates are made of white insulating foam, come with a lid (handy for conserving heat on cold nights) and they already have holes in the bottom for drainage. They're lightweight and durable enough to move around easily. You can get them by asking at the produce department of your local supermarket, which routinely discards such crates.

Grapes also arrive at the supermarket in wooden crates, so you may have to go back more than once before you hit the right day.

To put a crate to use as a hot bed, lay a porous rag over the drainage holes to keep the growing medium from falling out. Then put a thin layer of soil mix in the bottom, followed by your heating cable or mat (running the power cord out through one of the bottom holes). Finally, top off with 3 in. to 4 in. of soil mix. You are now ready to sow your seeds.

—John Hillbrand, Bass, AR

A carpenter-box planter and cold frame

Here in the vegetable garden at Cantigny, a public garden outside Chicago, we've designed an easy-to-build planter that doubles as a cold frame. The planter is in the shape of a carpenter's tool box, with a handle suspended above the plants from the two ends (see the drawing below). Our planter is much too heavy to lift, but the handle serves to support a sheet of clear, 4-mil to 6-mil polyethylene plastic, which we roll down to protect tender annuals or

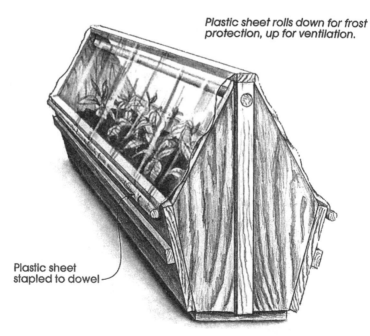

Plastic sheet rolls down for frost protection, up for ventilation.

Plastic sheet stapled to dowel

vegetables inside from spring or fall frosts, enclosing the planter like a cold frame. The design is simple and adaptable; you can vary the dimensions to fit your needs.

You don't need any special carpentry skills to build a carpenter-box planter. We made ours, which is 5 ft. long, about 2 ft. wide and a bit over 3 ft. tall, out of standard-size lumber, with the aid of a circular saw, a drill, a screwdriver and a hammer. We used yellow pine wood protected with an oil-based stain, and our box has held up well now for four years. The bottom of the planter is made of two 2x8s laid side by side, with a dozen ½-in. holes drilled for drainage; the sides are made of two 2x10s each; and the ends are cut from four 2x12 pieces. Two 2x4s keep the box off the ground. To reinforce the joints between the boards, we nailed in place strips of 1x3 trim. As a decorative touch, we tilted the sides outward at an angle, but you could just as easily keep them perpendicular to the base. Except for the trim, the box is held together by corrosion-resistant wood screws.

The handle of the planter is a 1¼-in.-diameter dowel. Because our planter sits in an exposed location, we soon found that we needed to fix the plastic to the box to keep the plastic from blowing away, so we added a 1x3 cap over the dowel and stapled the plastic to the cap. To make rolling the plastic up and down easy, we stapled the ends of the plastic to 1-in. dowels. When not in use, the rolled plastic rests on top of the cap.

–*Joseph R. Sable, Wheaton, IL*

Miniature cold frames

I've had great success in late winter and early spring germinating seeds of hardy plants, mainly primroses, in clear-plastic sweater boxes, the kind on sale for $8 or so at discount stores. I find the ones 16 in. long, 11 in. wide and 7 in. deep the handiest, but other sizes are available. The clear plastic admits light, and the close-fitting lid keeps conditions for germination ideally moist.

Before I stumbled on sweater boxes, I had hit-or-miss germination. I would sow seeds in packs or pots, set the containers outside and hope for favorable weather. The seeds were hardy and could stand freezes, but seedlings must never dry out, and after germination a sudden warm spell would often wipe out the crop of minute seedlings.

Now I sow seeds in packs and pots, as I did before, but I place the containers in the sweater box, atop a 1-in. layer of pebbles. I use rectangular and square containers rather than round pots because they fit better in a sweater box. I fill the containers almost to the top with seeding mix, sow seeds, add a thin layer of vermiculite to discourage damping off, water the containers well from the bottom and let them drain, and then put them in the box, where they remain evenly moist. When I'm short of space and the seeds haven't germinated yet, I stack the boxes. They have lugs on the bottom and matching depressions in the lid, so they stack sturdily.

Outdoors, sweater boxes act a bit like cold frames. I can remove the lid to allow air circulation and prevent overheating on warm, sunny days. Generally, once the seedlings are visible, I remove the lids and replace them only when a heavy rain threatens.

—*Sydney Eddison, Newtown, CT*

Plant starters

I've found an unusual and effective use for brown-paper grocery bags. They serve in my garden as in-ground plant containers, providing relief for transplants from competition with nearby plants, or allowing me to give a plant special soil.

I first came up with the idea when I wanted to transplant perennials into heavy meadow grass. I was afraid the soil would wash away if I cleared the grass, and I knew that the perennials would need help getting started. So I dug holes through the grass and placed double grocery bags (occasionally a single bag) in the holes. I turned the tops down twice, making cuffs that helped hold the bags open, and filled the bags with the soil from the holes, amended with peat, sand, bone meal and composted manure or sieved compost. I knew I'd have too little soil to fill the bags, so I put a layer of bulky stuff—wadded-up newspaper or handfuls of meadow grass—in the bags first. I set the transplants in the bags and watered them with a weak solution of fertilizer.

My idea worked beautifully. The cuffs offered a little shelter from wind, and the bags kept out the greedy grass roots until the perennials could make it on their own. The bags broke down in a few months—at least the cuffs fell apart by then—but that was long enough to make a difference.

The bags have proven to be a quick, reliable way to establish plants in tough conditions. They've worked equally well for me when I've added plants to established perennial beds or set out plants on a steep slope.

I've also found that I can amend the soil in the bags without affecting nearby plants. I can add gypsophila to an established flower bed with acid soil by liming the soil in the bag. I can start seeds of butterfly weed in the garden by sowing them in a bag filled with sandy soil. When I ran out of room in the garden last year, I sunk a bag in the garden path and started pumpkin seeds in it. The plants thrived.

—Connie Fitz, Woodstock, VT

Sowing small seeds

It seems a shame to waste seeds by thinning seedlings. I'd rather avoid thinning altogether by sowing the seeds at the right spacing. It's a tough job with small seeds, however. While fussing and fuming over a batch of dust-like foxglove seeds I was trying to sow in a flat, I happened upon a simple aid. I emptied the seeds onto a flat pane of glass (it was 4 in. by 10 in.). When I tipped the glass, I could easily slide the seeds around and control how they fell in the flat. For more precision, I could push individual seeds around between thumb and forefinger. This method allowed me to space the seeds evenly.

—Mark Trela, New Harmony, IN

Seed depth

When sowing seeds indoors or out, I've often been uncertain about how deep I actually planted them. Did that handful of soil cover the seeds to a depth of $\frac{1}{8}$ in., $\frac{1}{4}$ in. or somewhere in between? This year I eliminated all guesswork with garden stakes.

On each stake, I wrote the plant name and planting date, then drew two lines as far apart as the desired seed depth. When I placed each stake in the pot or garden, I pushed it in to the lower line. After I sowed seeds, I covered them so the potting mix or garden soil reached the upper line. Precision may not make a difference, but it can't hurt.

—Ellen M. Silva, Harrisonburg, VA

An easy way to propagate African violets

I've had good success propagating some of my favorite African violets in the clear plastic containers used to package the hydroponic lettuce that is sold at many grocery stores. I pinch a leaf off of the parent plant with my fingers and place the stem of the leaf in the small well in the bottom of the plastic container (see the drawing below). I fill the well with just enough water to touch the base of the leaf. Then I close the lid of the container and set it in a bright (but not sunny) window. The container acts as a tiny greenhouse for the cutting, maintaining high humidity (I have to add water to the well only about twice a month) and moderating air temperatures.

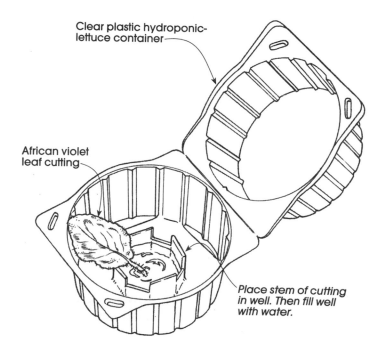

Clear plastic hydroponic-lettuce container

African violet leaf cutting

Place stem of cutting in well. Then fill well with water.

Roots begin to emerge from the leaf stem in about six to eight weeks. After two to three months, enough new leaves have emerged from the base of the cutting to transplant it to a small pot. I use a loose soil mix with a high proportion of perlite as a growing medium, and I water the pot by setting it in a tray of water in which I've mixed soluble African violet fertilizer according to directions. When my fragile cutting grows into a husky plant, I repot it and care for it as I do all of the other African violets in my collection.

–Marie L. Brinsfield, Ellicott City, MD

Propagating pachysandra

When I decided several years ago to plant pachysandra (*Pachysandra terminalis*) as a groundcover in two shady spots in my yard, I didn't run out to the garden center to buy flats of cuttings. I knew from my grandmother that it would be easy to start my own cuttings for free.

The propagation process was simple. With permission from my pachysandra-rich neighbor, I went next door with a laundry basket and snipped the tips (down to the first leaf juncture) off of about 200 to 300 shoots. I brought them home and stuck them, in bunches of 25, into wide-mouthed glass jars filled with water, and placed the jars in a shaded spot. (A pinch of water-soluble fertilizer seemed to help the rooting process along.) In three to four weeks, the cuttings had sprouted enough roots to be planted out.

Because the areas that I wanted the pachysandra to cover were large, it took a number of years for me to complete the project. About three times during the growing season, from April to August, I visited my neighbor's patch and came away with a full basket. Today, thanks to a little bit of effort on my part, I have my own thriving pachysandra patches.

–Martha McKeon, Sandy Hook, CT

Easy propagation of *Coreopsis rosea*

I have found an easy and non-disruptive way to propagate *Coreopsis rosea* at any time during the growing season. *C. rosea* is a small, pink, branching coreopsis that thrives in full sun as long as it has adequate moisture.

From an established plant I extract six or eight grasslike shoots by gently pulling each at its base. I then transplant these shoots at the new site by making holes in the earth several inches apart with a stick or pencil, inserting a shoot into each hole, firming the soil and watering it in.

I have propagated *C. rosea* in this way several times during the driest of summers here in the Northeast and have quite a few specimens that are now full enough to become donors themselves.

–Ed Temple, Brooklyn, NY

In-ground division of perennials

Dividing perennials doesn't have to be an arduous task. If you take just a little extra care with them, many of the tougher, fibrous-rooted plants (those with freely branching root systems, such as daylilies, hostas and ornamental grasses) can be cut into pieces while they're still in the ground. To do this, I use a sharp, flat-

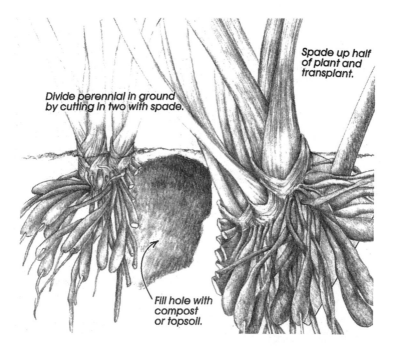

Spade up half of plant and transplant.

Divide perennial in ground by cutting in two with spade.

Fill hole with compost or topsoil.

bladed spade or a cultivating fork to cut or separate the crown in two. (Depending on the size and vigor of the plant, you can cut the crown into several smaller pieces the way you would a pie.) I dig around one half of the crown and pull it free for relocation elsewhere, leaving the other half in place (see the drawing on the facing page). Then I fill the hole with compost or top soil and water thoroughly.

I think this method has a couple of advantages over digging up the entire plant. To begin with, it's easier. You have to lift only part of the plant out of the ground. If you're working on a sizable specimen, this can save your back a lot of strain. In-ground division also spares the half left in place from much of the shock of being cut in two. While the piece you carry away may wilt and require cutting back, the piece in the ground rarely shows any signs of having just undergone major surgery. This allows you to undertake division in warm weather without marring your display.

–John Shaffer, Potomac, MD

A simpler way to separate daylilies

My husband's parents, members of the American Hemerocallis Society, saw me struggling one afternoon to separate a clump of daylilies I had just dug out of the ground. My mother-in-law instructed me to stand back; then she picked up a garden hose and washed all traces of dirt away. She gently rolled the newly clean tubers back and forth on the ground until they were all lying separately. The tubers were unharmed, the roots were long and straight, and the leaves showed no signs of abuse. Thanks to her, I no longer dread the task of separating daylilies—I just follow her lead and keep my garden hose handy.

–Mildred D. Brudd, Orland Park, IL

Growing Bulbs

Protecting spring bulbs with plastic pots

I used to plant my daffodils, tulips and other bulbs in the fall, enjoy the show the following spring, then forget about them when their leaves died down. All too often I was reminded of their location when, while doing some digging later in the season, I sliced through a group with my spade.

To protect my bulbs from accidental injury, I now set them inside plastic flower pots and plant the bulbs, pot and all, so that the rim of the pot rests just below soil level. I use the black plastic pots that nurseries sell their plants in; I usually have a stack of them around. The larger ones are about the right depth for most bulbs. I use a post hole digger (you could just as easily use a spade) to make the right size hole—three shovelsful is all it takes. I put about 3 in. of soil in the bottom of the pot, mix in fertilizer and place the bulbs on top. Then I set the pot in place and backfill the remaining soil into the pot. I haven't noticed any overcrowding due to multiplying bulbs. If I do, I'll just lift the pot and divide the bulbs.

Now if I hit a plastic pot when I'm digging, I know that there are bulbs nearby. As a bonus, gophers and moles can't get to bulbs protected by the pots.

—Jan Compton, Tahoe Paradise, CA

Homemade bulb planter

Instead of buying a bulb planter, I find that pieces of metal pipe make excellent tools to dig holes for bulbs. I use a hacksaw to cut the pipe to about a foot long. The pipe should be long enough so that when it's buried in the ground, there is enough pipe above the ground to pull out.

Using a hammer or mallet, or my hands if the soil is soft, I push the pipe into the ground to the planting depth of the bulb, and grab the section of pipe that is above the ground to pull it back out. The soil stays inside the pipe, making a neat hole in which to drop the bulb. Then I hold the pipe with the soil still inside it over the hole and tap the side with the mallet (see the drawing below). The soil falls back into the hole, covering the bulb.

—Arden Pischke, Ramsey, MN

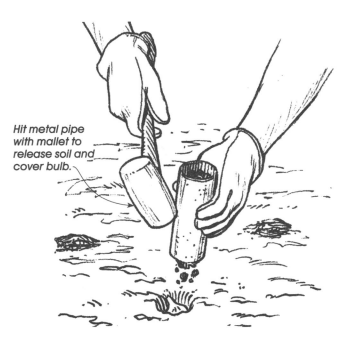

Hit metal pipe with mallet to release soil and cover bulb.

Encouraging forced hyacinths to stand tall

Hyacinths and other spring bulbs that are "forced" to bloom indoors in winter sometimes behave strangely. Rather than hold their flowers aloft, they open their blooms down in the leaves. You can encourage these dwarf flower stalks to elongate by covering the entire plant with an easy-to-make paper cone with a small opening at the top. After three or four days, the flower cluster stretches upward for the light.

Make the cone out of stiff, heavy paper that will block light; gift-box paper is ideal. Cut the paper into a rectangle, long enough so that, when rolled into a cone, it will fit inside the circumference of the pot. Leave an opening about ½ in. in diameter at the point, and hold it together with transparent or masking tape. Finally, trim the bottom so the cone will sit evenly in the pot (see the drawing below).

—Carol S. Tabb, Beaverton, OR

½ inch diameter

Adhesive tape

Remove cone when stem reaches for light—usually after three or four days.

Perennial tulips

For many gardeners, tulips can be a real disappointment. They often flower beautifully the first spring, then decline slowly each succeeding year until they manage to send up little more than a single fat leaf. Yet treating tulips as annuals, the way many public gardens do, is expensive and time-consuming.

You don't have to give up on tulips. If you plant the early flowering types and care for them as I suggest, you can have tulips that flower and increase for many years. I recommend kaufmanianas, fosterianas, greigiis, darwin hybrids and what bulb nurseries call "single early tulips" and "double early tulips." My early flowering tulips have been going strong for 15 years.

Here is my tulip-care regimen. I plant the bulbs in the fall at a depth of 6 in. to 7 in. in well-drained, slightly acid soil. In early November, December, January and February—weather permitting—I fertilize with 10-10-10 (proportion of nitrogen, phosphorus, potassium) fertilizer at a rate of about one handful per square yard (you may find that you get good results with less fertilizer). After the tulips bloom in spring, I remove the spent flowers promptly so that the bulbs put all their energy into making new flower buds for the following year's bloom. I leave the foliage in place until it turns yellow—about a month after the plants have flowered.

—Michael J. Zajic, Washington, DC

One hole for several small bulbs

Masses of minor bulbs, such as crocuses or glory-of-the-snow (*Chionodoxa*), are beautiful naturalized in lawn areas as well as garden beds. I've found an easy way to plant these bulbs without digging a hole through the grass for each one. I use a bulb planter to pull out a plug of sod, taking care not to dig too deep. Because these bulbs are so tiny, I can easily fit several of them into one hole. I then put the sod plug back in. In the spring, the bulbs come up through the grass in clusters.

—Duncan Brine, Pawling, NY

Amaryllis bulbs like the refrigerator
My amaryllis bulbs flourish on my patio during the summer and go dormant in the autumn. The first time I brought the dormant bulbs indoors in November, the warmth of my house seemed to make the bulbs think spring had arrived. Although I stored them in a dark closet, they began to grow even without light or water.

I knew I had to keep the bulbs cool but not frozen. A garage or basement would have been ideal, but I had neither available to me. The only possibility was the refrigerator. To save space, I took the bulbs out of their pots, shook off some of the soil and put them in plastic bags with plenty of air holes. I then placed them in paper bags to keep the refrigerator clean. In spring, the bulbs seemed to take longer than usual to sprout, but I was rewarded with fine flowers at Easter.

–Barbara Dege, Hackensack, NJ

Monitor bulbs with vented plastic bags
To store bulbs for next season, I put them in vented plastic vegetable bags and hang them in my garage, which receives some light and has good air circulation. I write any pertinent information directly on the bags. This method makes it easy for me to monitor the condition of the bulbs visually so I'll know when to plant them.

–Ruby Thomas, Anacortes, WA

Coding stored bulbs
I have found a simple way to code the flower color of the dahlia bulbs and begonia tubers that I save over the winter. I buy a bag of rubber bands in mixed colors and slip a rubber band of the appropriate color around each bulb or tuber. If I can't match the flower color, I use a rubber band of a non-floral color, such as tan, green or black, and record the flower color and rubber-band color together on a piece of paper.

–William J. Schneider, Suffern, NY

Bulb planter

If you're tired of troweling deep holes for bulbs, you might want to try the heavy-duty planting tool that landscape contractors use. Built like a spade with a tube instead of a blade, it lets you cut and lift a cylindrical plug of soil anywhere from 2 in. to 10 in. deep. Best of all, you stand upright and let your legs and weight do the work.

A co-worker and I built our own planting tool. You can, too, if you have a welding torch, or you can order a manufactured bulb planter from a garden center. For the tube, we cut a 2½-in. by 10-in. length of copper pipe with a 45° angle on one end, as the drawing at right shows. For the handle and shaft, we brazed together two pieces of ½-in. galvanized pipe. (You could make the handle with a ½-in. threaded tee and two 4-in. nipples instead.) For the foot bar, we cut an 8-in. length of 1½-in. angle iron and bolted and brazed it to the shaft. Finally, we brazed the copper tube to the shaft. I've used the tool to plant hundreds of bulbs and it works great.

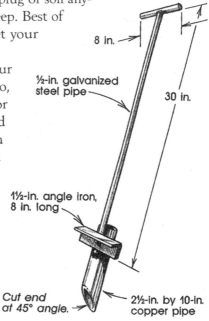

8 in.

½-in. galvanized steel pipe

30 in.

1½-in. angle iron, 8 in. long

Cut end at 45° angle.

2½-in. by 10-in. copper pipe

–Kenneth Elder, Sewell, NJ

Outdoor containers of spring bulbs

With a little bit of planning, it's possible to have a spectacular container display of spring bulbs outdoors—even in a cold-winter climate. The secret is to plant individual bulbs in small pots in the fall, overwinter them in the ground and then transplant them—pot and all—into the larger container in the spring.

Preparing for a spring container is easy. Fill the desired number of smaller pots (plastic or peat pots 2 in. to 3 in. in diameter and 3 in.

to 4 in. deep are ideal) to the brim with soilless mix. Set the bulbs—one bulb per pot—on top of the mix. Then dig a trench 8 in. or 10 in. deep in an out-of-the-way corner of the yard. Put the pots side by side in the trench, sprinkle bulb fertilizer over them, water and fill the trench with a 6-in. layer of fallen leaves or pine needles to insulate the bulbs from temperature fluctuations and to make it easy to exhume the pots.

In the spring, begin checking for top growth when you see that similar sorts of bulbs in the garden have begun to sprout above ground. Potted bulbs with about 2 in. of growth are ready for transplanting. (The emerging leaves will be white because of light deprivation, but they will green up quickly once you take them out from under the leaves.) Fill the larger container with soil mix, and sink the potted bulbs so that they sit just below soil level.

The variety of bulb displays is limitless. You can combine different types of bulbs that flower at the same time or organize succession plantings. It's easy to pop out plants that are fading and pop in others that are coming on strong.

After a bulb has flowered, you can move it into the garden for future enjoyment. Just remove the bulb carefully from its pot (peat pots can go directly into the ground) and plant it to the normal depth.

—Brent Heath, Gloucester, VA

Enjoying tulips

I have some tips that can make growing tulips more rewarding. Many gardeners dislike the sight of aging tulip leaves, but with planning you can minimize their impact. First, use small groupings—no more than 24 bulbs. Even 10 plants produce a delightful spot of color. Set the groups throughout the garden, with perennial plants close by to fill in and hide the waning tulip foliage. Bearded irises are ideal plants. Other good choices include Dutchman's-breeches, squirrel corn, trillium, wild blue phlox, wild geranium and Virginia bluebell. All are large enough to screen the tulips, and all flower attractively as the tulips decline.

Planting tulip bulbs deeply helps avoid losses to rodents. Some gardeners complain that squirrels eat bulbs. Actually, squirrels burying nuts for the winter accidentally dislodge tulip bulbs that have been planted shallowly. Mice, chipmunks and voles will eat bulbs, but they cause very little trouble with tulips that are planted 8 in. to 10 in. deep.

–John W. Smith, Grand Rapids, MI

Safe fall digging

Every fall, I add more bulbs to my garden. Most of the bulbs I planted in other years are invisible in fall, lying dormant underground. I avoid slicing into them accidentally because among them I grow a marker, a bulb that grows in fall, the grape hyacinth (*Muscari armeniacum*). There are other *Muscari* species commonly called grape hyacinths, but only the *armeniacum* species is green in fall. The leaves appear in early autumn, before it's time to plant bulbs, and they persist over winter. Cobalt-blue flowers appear in spring, and the plant goes dormant in summer. It is hardy in Zones 4-9.

I know one other plant that can mark bulb plantings in fall, but it is less versatile than *M. armeniacum*. The Madonna lily (*Lillium candidum*) leafs out in fall, too. The plants are big and showy, however—not as suited to keeping company with tulips and daffodils as the 8-in.-tall grape hyacinth is. Also, Madonna lilies must be planted in late summer, while you can plant the grape hyacinth in fall, at the same time as the bulbs it will mark.

–Judy Wells, Shawnee Mission, KS

Making room for more tulips

I always have a hard time finding a place to plant new tulip bulbs because I'm afraid of splitting bulbs that are already in the ground.

My job has become easier since I came up with a great idea: I dig holes in the spring while the tulip foliage is dying. In between the recently bloomed tulips I plant gladiolus bulbs. In the fall, after the gladiola have finished blooming, I dig them up and replace them with tulip bulbs for the following spring.

–Betty McRainey, Euclid, OH

Forcing bulbs

I like color and fragrance indoors during the winter, so every fall I prepare a good number of bulbs for forcing. People who store bulbs in a cold frame or a refrigerator and then pot them for forcing are sometimes rewarded with wan plants and blasted buds. With my method, the bulbs produce a full system of roots before the tops grow, so the plants develop strong leaves and flowers.

In the fall, I buy bulbs of hyacinths, narcissus and single early tulips. Shortly after leaf fall, before the ground freezes, I pot the bulbs. Then I pack the pots in a plastic laundry basket or crate, set everything in a safe spot outdoors, and rake leaves 2½ ft. deep on top. I've always used oak leaves, which don't mat. If you use softer leaves, cover them with a sheet of plastic so they won't get too soggy. During the next two months or so, I check the pots periodically and keep them moist. The bulbs strike roots and are ready to come indoors in 10 to 12 weeks—the sure sign is roots showing out of the bottom of a pot. By then, the tops are also growing and are usually an inch or two tall. I put the pots in a cool (50° to 60°F), bright spot and the plants respond with vigorous growth. More heat forces growth too fast.

If the weather cooperates, I like to prolong the season by bringing the pots indoors in succession. In the fall and early winter, I've seen nighttime temperatures go as low as -20°F without harming the bulbs outdoors. But later, when the soil under the pile freezes and the days are colder, the same temperature would probably kill the bulbs. My experience is limited to USDA Zone 5 and south. North of Zone 5, you'd probably need to get the last bulbs indoors before mid-December.

—Steven Frowine, Lansdale, PA

Gravel protects bulbs from voles

Here at the Daffodil Mart, a bulb nursery in Virginia, and in many other parts of the country, voles are one of the biggest pests of bulbs. Voles—small rodents distinguished from mice by their short tails—often tunnel just beneath the surface of the soil and devour bulbs; tulips in particular are a delicacy. I've found that a handful of sharp, crushed gravel or marble chips poured over a bulb at planting time helps deter voles (see the drawing on the facing page). Voles

56

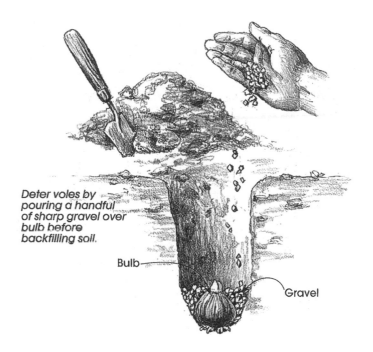

Deter voles by pouring a handful of sharp gravel over bulb before backfilling soil.

Bulb

Gravel

dislike hard, gravelly soil. Rather than dig through the gravel, they'll look elsewhere for their food. And because voles don't dig deep into the soil, it also helps to plant bulbs deep. Tulips, for example, should be planted 10 in. to 12 in. below the surface of the soil.

– Brent Heath, Gloucester, VA

Rodent-proofing tulips

Until last year, if I fall-planted tulip bulbs, before spring I lost them in great numbers to the rodents that overwinter under the mulch in my perennial border. (I don't know which to blame, but I have mice, voles and moles.) I tried moth balls as a deterrent, with no success. Then last year I planted tulip bulbs in buried baskets, and every bulb came through the winter unscathed.

I set out to make cages of wire mesh, but instead came home from the hardware store with six small plastic baskets, each 12 in. by 9 in. by 4½ in. deep. They had mesh sides and a solid bottom,

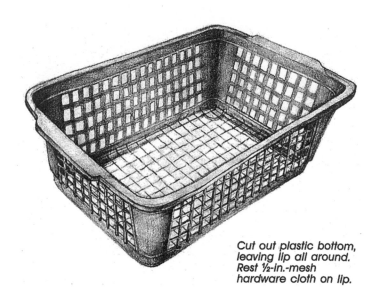

*Cut out plastic bottom,
leaving lip all around.
Rest ½-in.-mesh
hardware cloth on lip.*

and I cut out the bottom with a knife and replaced it with a rectangle of ½-in. mesh hardware cloth (see the drawing above). Each basket took less than five minutes to prepare, and held five large tulip bulbs.

I loosened the soil, incorporating peat moss and bone meal, and set the baskets as deep as I dared, with their rims 1 in. below ground level. Most authorities say tulip bulbs should be planted 6 in. to 8 in. deep, but, to my eye, those in the baskets grew just as well as bulbs I planted 8 in. deep the year before. I'm sure the baskets would work equally well for crocus bulbs, which are usually planted 4 in. deep.

Although a wire cage would work, too, I like the baskets. They won't cut you if you forget where they are while transplanting or cultivating, they're easy to prepare and they're widely available. Mine cost about 75¢ each and I had a choice of several colors. I bought the dark brown. That way, even if an edge becomes visible, it won't show.

—Sydney Eddison, Newtown, CT

Parking tulips

I liked Sydney Eddison's tips about planting tulip bulbs in buried plastic baskets to protect them from hungry rodents. I think the baskets would be great for people who are eager to get tulips out of the garden when the foliage turns unsightly, or who want the space for annuals. Once the blooms have peaked, you could dig up the whole basket and, without disturbing foliage or bulbs, replant in an out-of-the-way place and mark the spot. In the fall, when the annuals succumb to frost, you can move the basket back.

—Karen A. Krueger, Green Bay, WI

Sydney Eddison replies: Tulips will send their roots well beyond the baskets I use, which are 9 in. by 12 in. by 4½ in. deep. If you intend to move the plants, you should bury larger, deeper baskets, which you can lift with all the roots.

Squirrel-proofing bulbs

Chipmunks, squirrels and other rodents love to dig up and devour many kinds of spring-flowering bulbs—tulips are a particular favorite. I've found that wrapping bulbs in chicken-wire mesh before planting deters rodents (see the drawing at right). The shoots and roots can grow through the wires, but the critters can't reach the bulb. Because wrapping the bulbs is a bit time-consuming, I protect only my most prized acquisitions. The others have to take their chances.

—Robert Benoit, Centre Harbor, NH

Plant Care

Leave snow on bent branches

Gardeners often worry that heavy snow will snap tree or shrub branches or cause them to bend out of shape. Here at the Minnesota Extension Service we advise them in most cases to leave well enough alone. If temperatures are much below freezing, the wood will be brittle. In the attempt to help a tree or shrub by scraping or shoveling off snow, you're actually running the risk of breaking branches yourself.

Most winter-hardy woody plants are adapted to carrying the weight of snow. During warmer weather in spring, trees and shrubs whose branches have become splayed start to come back into shape. If you fear that a prized plant won't recover in good form, you can tie stems together to give temporary support—just wait until temperatures are above freezing and the snow has melted or fallen off before you bend branches. Remember to remove the ties once spring is well under way.

—Deborah Brown, St. Paul, MN

Clothespins open up trees

Cherries and other trees with upright habits need to have their branches spread apart when young to make a strong, open framework. I've found that two spring-type clothespins with their "mouths" clamped together make the perfect device for spreading young branches (see the drawing below).

—Diane Cary, Winters, CA

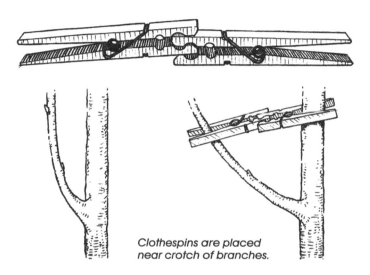

Clothespins are placed
near crotch of branches.

Assembly-line fertilizing for annuals

Since most summer annuals benefit from frequent liquid fertilizing, anything that speeds up the chore of fertilizing these annuals is welcome. I line up plastic 1-gal. milk jugs that I have accumulated, and put the required amount of fertilizer concentrate for 1 gal. of water into each one. I then fill up each of the containers with water in an assembly-line fashion. With several containers of fertilizer ready to go, the amount of time it takes to fertilize is greatly reduced, leaving me with more time to enjoy the garden.

—Robert H. Nelson, Seattle, WA

Broadcasting dry chemicals by hand

When I need to apply granular fertilizers, herbicides or insecticides on small areas and grades too steep or rough for a drop spreader, I use plastic flower pots, the kind with four holes around the edge of the bottom and no center hole. I put one pot inside another and twist them so that the holes overlap only slightly. Then I fill the inner pot with the granules and walk the plot, gently jiggling the pots to filter the material out through the holes. I get surprisingly even coverage, especially if I adjust the holes for a light flow and walk the area twice in opposing directions. There's no way to calibrate this applicator, so I measure the plot and weigh the granules before starting. If I have granules left after walking the plot, I just keep going over the area until they're gone.

—*Tom Vasale, Charleston, WV*

Garden-chemical storage

I've found a new use for old, defunct refrigerators—they make excellent cupboards for garden chemicals. The tight seal around the door keeps granular and powdered fertilizers, insecticides and herbicides dry, and contains the noxious odors they can emit. Before we put garden chemicals into our old refrigerator, I suffered from persistent headaches. I'm convinced that our home heating and cooling systems circulated the odors from chemicals stored in the basement throughout the house. Once the chemicals were contained inside the refrigerator, the headaches stopped.

If children have access to your old refrigerator, keep it locked with a padlock and chain. It's a good idea to keep pesticides under lock and key anyway, whether there are children around or not.

—*Mrs. Robert Lauderdale, Lexington, KY*

An easy haircut for grass clumps

After enjoying the beautiful stalks of ornamental grass through the winter, I have an easy and quick way to deadhead them in early spring.

I wrap a bungee cord around the clumps and trim with a chain saw. Since we have quite a few clumps, this is very convenient.

—Gregory J. Wojick, Greenwich, CT

Weight training for fruit trees

The inclination of an apple branch affects its fruitfulness. Upright branches tend to remain vegetative; horizontal branches tend to bear fruit. While shoots are young and limber, they can be trained to a desirable angle, given a bit of ingenuity. Orchardists pull them down with twine tied to stakes, weight them with bags of sand, or spread them with toothpicks wedged between shoot and trunk.

I spotted a new training gadget in Europe a few years ago, made some of my own and liked them. I use them in the orchards at

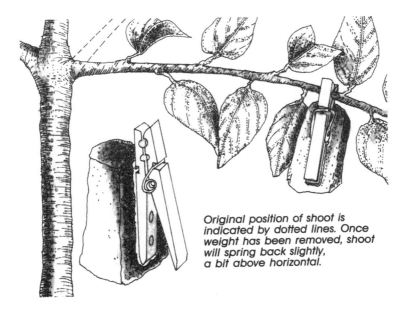

Original position of shoot is indicated by dotted lines. Once weight has been removed, shoot will spring back slightly, a bit above horizontal.

Penn State, where I'm a pomologist. They're inexpensive, easily made, durable and effective—worth trying.

The gadget is a 4-oz. weight glued to a wooden, spring-type clothespin (see the drawing on the previous page). I mass-produce uniform weights by filling standard bedding-plant six-packs with a mixture of water and portland cement (no sand). When the cement has set, I pull off the six-pack and fasten a clothespin to each weight with a bead of Liquid Nails. I drill holes in one leg of the clothespin before gluing—glue pushes into the holes and strengthens the bond.

I generally hang the weights in early- to mid-summer, when shoots begin to stiffen at the base and can bear some strain, though I've also changed branch angles in winter. Where to hang the weights and how long to leave them on is a matter of common sense, but don't simply arch shoots. It's better to move a weight toward the base of the shoot and reset the angle with gentle hand pressure. On stiff shoots, use more than one weight. Fixing a new angle takes a few days to two weeks or more.

–L.D. Tukey, University Park, PA

Letting Mother Nature do the gardening

Gardeners work hard to get nature to do their bidding, but nature can sometimes make a beautiful garden by itself, without any help from humans. We discovered this phenomenon after we poured our concrete driveway. When the work was done, there remained a 2-ft.-wide strip of hard clay denuded of topsoil along one side of the drive. Because we planned to put in a basketball standard, we decided not to plant the strip. Instead, we filled the space with cobblestones to prevent basketballs from splashing in the mud.

The results surprised us. The first year we did get a few weeds, but the next year we saw some Johnny-jump-ups. The following season, perennial verbena appeared, then snow-in-summer, snapdragons, catmint and some old-fashioned flowers that I used to see in my grandmother's garden. People began to stop and ask how I grew such pretty flowers among rocks.

I decided never to plant or rearrange things in the strip. I thin only if a plant is covering its neighbor. Occasionally, I pull a particularly aggressive weed. I water once a month if we don't get rain.

If you have a little spot of ground that you find a bit difficult to tend, consider just sitting back and letting Mother Nature do the gardening for you there.

—Bonnie Wadley, Lehi, UT

More phlox flowers

I've discovered that timely deadheading of summer phlox (*Phlox paniculata*) can extend its bloom season. After the first flush of bloom—which comes in July, August or September, depending on the cultivar—I cut off the top 10 in. to 20 in. from the flower-bearing stems. In a few days, new growth appears, and another round of white, pink or purple flowers is soon on the way. You can encourage more than one extra round of flowering; I often have phlox flowers open until frost. The subsequent flower clusters are not as large or as full as the first ones, but phlox flowers are always welcome in my garden, and they look great with late-blooming perennials such as asters.

—Martha Janik, Springfield, MA

Roses love bananas

By now everyone knows that roses love banana skins. However, I have found an easier way to use them without disturbing the roots or burying the skins so shallow that rodents dig them up. I just use my garden shears and snip, snip, snip every quarter of an inch across the skins. Throughout the year, I sprinkle the chopped-up skins on my roses. The winter cold and summer sun will turn the skins black in a day and you'll never see them again, but your roses will benefit from the precious minerals.

—Florence Edwards Wagner, Athens, OH

Annual succession

With the temperature and humidity both hitting the 90s, summer in Florida (which starts in March and lasts at least until October) is no time to be expending any more energy than necessary in the garden. I've discovered a trick that gives me new pots of annuals to keep up the color show over our endless growing season.

To start succeeding generations of such readily self-seeding annuals as vinca and impatiens, I fill a pot of the desired size with soil mix and tuck it under the canopy of a large pot of these annuals in flower. Their seeds fall into the lower pot and begin to sprout in a few weeks, but I leave the pot next to the mother plant until the seedlings fill in. Then I move the young plants where I want them, or I grow them on for eventual transplanting.

—Bobbie Meyers, Palm Beach Gardens, FL

Attracting bees

Last year I observed firsthand how bees can improve the yield of a garden crop. I planted borage in several spots in the garden, and the flowers of this easily grown annual herb attracted a much greater number of bees than I usually see. They seem to have visited other plants, too. My pole beans, which were close to the borage, produced straight, well-filled pods, with none of the pinched, curved pods that result from poor seed set. In the past, I've found four or five seeds in the pods I save for the following year's crop. Last year I commonly found nine seeds per pod. I intend to make successive sowings of borage in the garden next year, so I'll have flowers for most of the growing season.

—Lon Rombough, Aurora, OR

Plants survive winter under Styrofoam cooler

When polystyrene picnic coolers go on sale at the end of the summer, I buy several for protecting marginally hardy plants from our brutal winters. In late fall, I turn coolers upside down over plants in need of protection and weight the coolers down with a rock. This technique has helped me to overwinter small, newly planted trees and young rhododendrons. It has been especially effective for roses. I hill a few inches of dry manure over the graft of each rose, prune back the canes and set a cooler over the bush. The roses come through the winter with less dieback than with any other method I've tried.

I place the cooler lids over the cut stems of perennials that are borderline hardy for my area. The polystyrene has allowed me to overwinter perennials rated one USDA Hardiness Zone warmer than the one in which I live.

—Laurel Perga, Joliet, MT

Rescuing neglected garden gems

Abandoned home sites can be a treasure trove of tough perennials and shrubs. As a bonus, many of the plants you discover there are difficult or impossible to find in commerce today. With care, you can bring them home to start a new life in your garden.

Here's my equipment for plant-hunting. For small and medium-sized plants, I bring 4-in. nursery pots and 1-lb. and 3-lb. coffee cans. For the root balls of larger plants, I bring newspapers. I bring gloves, pruning shears (for cuttings), baby food jars (for seed collecting) and several large soda bottles filled with water. On the way out, I grab a trowel, a shovel and my hat.

When you dig up plants in active growth, leave as much soil around their roots as possible. Place plants immediately into pots, water them and then move them into the shade. On a hot day, a sprinkling of water on the foliage seems to help reduce transplant shock. Set plants too big for pots on several sheets of newspaper. Wet the roots and fold the paper to cover the entire root ball.

Ask permission before you set out to collect and transplant foundlings. Old garden gems are more than worth the effort.

—Jane Martin, Monahans, TX

Early blooming companions for hostas

Hostas are slow to emerge in spring. While other perennials are busy sending up new shoots, hostas take their time unfurling their heart-shaped leaves, so the area surrounding the plants tends to look bare until they've filled in.

One way to achieve a fuller look earlier in the season is to plant spring wildflowers such as Virginia bluebells (*Mertensia virginica*) and bloodroot (*Sanguinaria canadensis*) around hostas (see the drawing below). The wildflowers come up early and flower before the hostas fill in, then go dormant under the canopy of hosta leaves. Quite by chance, I have found that epimediums, which slowly spread to form a delicate ground cover, also make good companions for hostas. Epimediums open their spurred flowers at the same time as the spring wildflowers do, and they survive in full vigor despite the dense shade cast by the hostas.

–Lucy Fuchs, Ambler, PA

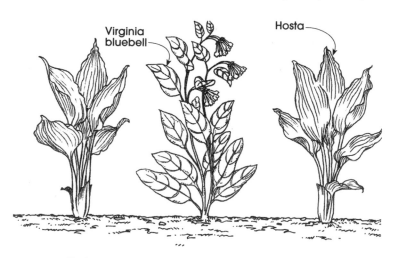

Virginia bluebell

Hosta

Spring wildflowers emerge from ground and bloom before tardy hostas fully unfurl their leaves.

Overwintering roots in perlite

Soon after the first frost, I dig up my amaranth (*Gomphrena*) herbs, separate the plants, and trim off the stems and leaves. I fill a plastic dishpan one-third full of perlite, put the roots in and cover them with more perlite. I store the roots in a dark, cool cellar, keeping them slightly damp during the winter. In early March, the plants can be replanted in plastic pots and kept indoors. In May, my amaranths are ready to go back in the ground outside. The plants at this point are much more established than seedlings would be and are ready to harvest in a month.

–Mildred Recchil, Newfield, NJ

Dusting

To clean dirt and dust off fuzzy-leafed plants such as purple passion and African violet (which hates water on its leaves), I use a baby's hairbrush and gently stroke the dust off the leaves.

–Claudia Allen, Newtown, CT

Milk for shiny houseplant leaves

When I want the leaves of houseplants, such as philodendron, to shine, I take a cotton ball and moisten it with a little milk—it doesn't matter whether it's regular, skim or acidopholis. The milk removes water spots from hard water and shines up the leaves, without harming the plants.

–Judy Showers, Carlisle, PA

Watering the Garden

Rain catchers

After quite a bit of head-scratching, we cobbled up a system that stores rainwater for the garden. Each downspout on our house now runs to two barrels connected by a piece of plastic pipe. When the first barrel is full, the overflow spills through the pipe to the second barrel (see the drawing on the facing page). When both barrels are full, a length of downspout carries off the overflow. We installed bibbs near the base of each barrel so that we can hook up a hose and have gravity deliver the water to the garden.

The construction is rough and ready. We used old whiskey barrels, which cost $10 each. We cut some in half, drilled holes in their bottoms for drainage, filled them with dirt and sand, and used them as pedestals for the other barrels. If your garden is below your house, you can dispense with pedestals and set the barrels on the ground. Drill a hole at the base of each barrel and press in the hose bibb. Make the hole a tight fit and caulk the bibb. Fill the barrels with water and let them stand for several days so that the staves can swell and seal the joints. The barrels will settle a few inches,

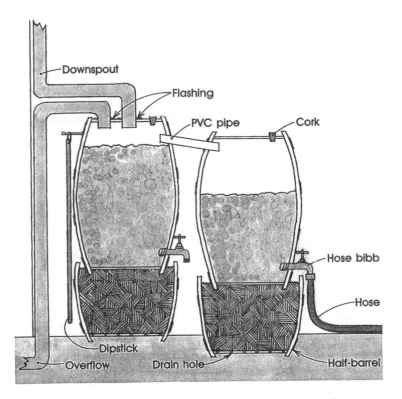

Downspout

Flashing

PVC pipe

Cork

Hose bibb

Hose

Dipstick

Overflow

Drain hole

Half-barrel

too. Then cut two holes in the top of the first barrel, one for the incoming downspout, one for the overflow downspout. We screwed and caulked two fitted pieces of aluminum flashing over the holes to seal the downspouts. Run the overflow downspout to the same outlet or spillway that the original downspout used. Then drill a hole near the top of the first barrel and a slightly lower hole in the second barrel, and run a length of plastic pipe between the two. Make the holes a tight fit. As a final touch, we drilled l-in. holes in the top of each barrel so that we could check the water level with a dipstick. Between checks, we keep the dipstick holes corked.

If all goes well, you'll have about 55 gal. of free water per barrel. We connect either a regular garden hose or a soaker hose to the barrels and get a slow, welcome stream of sour-mash-smelling water.

–Fannie Schubert, Atlanta, GA

Rolling rain barrels

There's something special about rainwater; plants seem to prefer it to what comes out of the tap. Here in southern California, where water of any sort is hard to come by, we get almost all of our rain during the winter. To make the most of what little rain we get,

Plastic garbage can

2×4's

Casters

I've come up with a system that uses heavy-duty, plastic garbage cans for catching and storing water running off the roof of our shed. Each can sits on a flat, wooden dolly that rolls on casters (see the drawing above). Because the garden shed in our backyard sits on a concrete pad that extends well beyond the foundation, I can roll cans full of water away from the roof line and roll empty cans into place to catch more rain. Most years, I can fill nine or ten 32-gal. cans this way. If you have a level concrete or asphalt driveway, you can try my technique.

The dollies are very easy to make. Purchase one 8-ft. 2x4 for each dolly. (I used rot-resistant redwood; pressure-treated wood will work just as well.) Cut five 18-in. lengths from the 2x4. Two of the lengths serve as cross pieces; the other three rest on top—one at each end of the cross pieces and one centered in the middle. Fix the wood together with $2\frac{1}{2}$-in. galvanized wood screws turned in to pre-drilled holes (you can also use bolts). Then screw four 2-in. casters (the kind that pivot with the aid of ball bearings) into the cross pieces, one at each end.

One garbage can looks pretty much like another, but I've found that Rubbermaid cans are more durable. The less expensive cans I bought developed fine splits along their seams and began to leak.

In between rains and after filling, cover the garbage cans with their lids to prevent evaporation and to keep out insects and debris. To deliver collected water to plants, you can set up a pump or a siphon. I just take a bucket and plunge it into the barrel.

—Charles Stein, Arcadia, CA

Vacation from watering

To prevent potted plants from drying out when no one can water them, put each pot into a plastic bag and tie the bag (not too tightly) around the neck of the plant, so that the entire pot is encased but the plant is not. If possible, stop fertilizer a month beforehand. Water thoroughly and let the pot drain before bagging it, and then keep it in a cool, sheltered place. Bagged pots can be left, without watering, for several weeks.

—Joyce Descloux, Randolph, NJ

Deep watering

I got frustrated watering my raised vegetable beds by hand. If I tried to hurry things along, water ran off the beds, and if I slowed down, I spent more time than I liked on watering. I experimented with simple alternatives to hand watering and found a good one— letting water seep from small holes in 5-gal. plastic buckets. I can fill the buckets in far less time than I used to spend hand watering, and once the buckets are filled, my work is done.

The buckets are easy to find. Many products are sold in them: driveway sealer, paint, drywall joint compound, pool chemicals and so on. I get mine free at construction sites.

Preparing and using the buckets is straightforward. I punch about ten holes around the lower half and in the bottom of each bucket, using a hammer and a small chisel. A drill and bit would do the job, too. I bury the buckets with their tops just above ground level. I started out leaving the buckets empty, but I was afraid they might overheat the surrounding soil. Now I put large rocks in the bottom half of the buckets, and fill the top half with compost to several inches from the rim. I've found that this arrangement holds about 4 gal. of water, which I can dump in all at once from another bucket, or run in from a hose in a few minutes. The water drains through the compost, picking up nutrients as it goes, and trickles through the holes into the soil. The bucket takes about five minutes to empty, and all the water stays in the bed. How far the water spreads depends on the soil, but roots tend to grow toward the water. I decide when to rewater by the look of the plants and the feel of the soil a few inches down.

Buckets take very little room. In a bed 4½ ft. wide and 22 ft. long, I space five buckets evenly along the centerline. The bed covers 99 sq. ft. and the buckets subtract less than 4 sq. ft. I find them barely noticeable (though my wife thinks they're unsightly). Only the rims show, and when plants fill the bed, the buckets almost disappear.

I think the results repay the effort of preparing and burying the buckets, and more than make up for the space the buckets take. I use buckets mainly for thirsty crops, such as melons, tomatoes and squash. The plants produce significantly higher yields now than when I watered by hand. There are several reasons for the difference, I think. The plants get a light feeding with every watering, and very little water evaporates, which helps keep the soil constantly moist.

–Stephen Kennedy, Orrtanna, PA

Artificially moist sites

Even though I don't have a pond, and my soil is often dry, I've discovered how to grow plants that like wet feet, such as yellow flag iris *(Iris pseudacorus)* and sweet flag *(Acorus calamus)* without unusual quantities of water. The trick is to establish an artificially high water table by burying a container in the soil.

First, I learn about the plant I want to grow—the horizontal and downward spread of its roots, the amount of moisture it prefers, the sort of soil it requires. Next, I find a watertight container suited to the type and number of plants I want to grow; it might be an old wading pool, a plastic garbage can, a plastic tarp or a pond liner.

I dig the hole and seat the container. Then I amend the excavated soil to meet the requirements of the plant in question. Before I refill the hole, I stand a small-diameter (1½-in.) pipe toward the back of the container to serve as a dipstick tube (see the drawing below). The pipe, which can be made of stainless steel, PVC or any

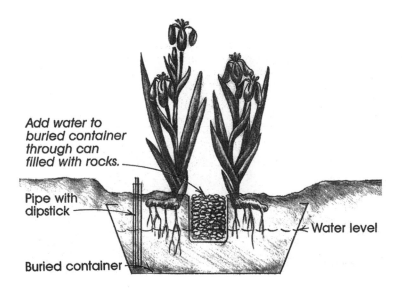

Add water to buried container through can filled with rocks.

Pipe with dipstick

Water level

Buried container

other corrosion-resistant material, should be flush with the bottom of the container and rise a couple of inches above the eventual soil level. I fill in around the pipe, watering as I go to settle the soil, and stop at a level below that of the surrounding ground. The resulting depression will help to catch rainwater and reduce the need for irrigation. Now I'm ready to plant, mulch and water.

To ease watering and to prevent erosion, I punch pea-sized holes in a coffee can, fill it with rocks to keep debris out, and sink it up to its rim in the wet area. When the dipstick (a dowel) shows that the water level has fallen to 8 in. below soil level, I water through the can until the area begins to flood.

–*Ronald L. Carrow, Omaha, NE*

Routing rainwater from roof to soaker hose

The extended drought that parched California until last winter inspired my wife and me to devise ways to catch every raindrop—especially the raindrops that run off the roof. So we came up with a variation on the traditional rain barrel. Rather than catching and holding roof runoff, our barrel is designed to leak. Standard plumbing parts allow us to route water from a small hole cut at the base of the barrel through a garden hose to soaker hoses laid near plants that thrive on extra moisture.

There are probably many ways of making a leaky rain barrel. I'll tell you how I made ours, using parts that I had on hand, but you, or a knowledgeable salesperson at a well-stocked hardware or plumbing-supply store, may come up with a different way of fashioning one. Whatever parts you use, make sure they are made of corrosion-resistant materials—galvanized steel, stainless steel, brass or plastic.

I started by cutting a hole about ¾ in. in diameter at the base of a 32-gal. plastic trash barrel with a sharp pocket knife. Over the hole, I put flanges with threads for a ¾-in. pipe—one flange on the inside of the barrel and one on the outside. Two 1-in.-long stove bolts pushed through holes drilled in the barrel hold the flanges in place. Then, into each flange, I screwed ¾-in. pipe nipples—short sections of pipe threaded on both ends. To the nipple on the inside of the barrel, I attached a strainer I made from ⅛-in. galvanized mesh and held it in place with wire. I then screwed a pipe-to-hose

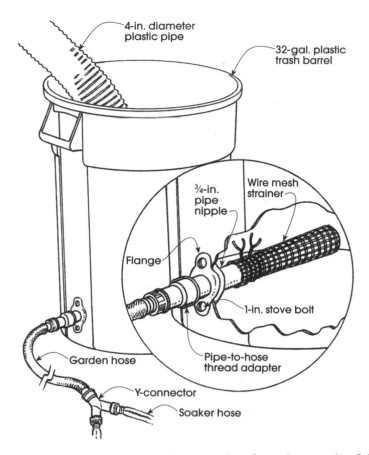

4-in. diameter plastic pipe

32-gal. plastic trash barrel

¾-in. pipe nipple

Wire mesh strainer

Flange

1-in. stove bolt

Garden hose

Pipe-to-hose thread adapter

Y-connector

Soaker hose

threaded adapter to the nipple protruding from the outside of the barrel so that I could attach a garden hose to the nipple (see the drawing above).

Our rainwater distribution system worked quite well. The water runs off the roof down a 4-in.-diameter pipe and into the barrel, then passes through the garden hose to two soaker hoses (the flat, plastic kind with pinprick holes) that branch off the garden hose from a Y-connector. To make sure the water runs out of the barrel, I elevated it on a sturdy wooden crate. I leave the ends of the soaker hoses open to reduce the likelihood that the barrel will overflow, but even if it does there's no harm done because our barrel sits in a bed of moisture-loving plants.

–H.W. Flesher, Modesto, CA

Spot fertilizing through drip irrigation

Most drip irrigation systems allow you to fertilize all of the plants with the same amount of fertilizer at the same time. But plants don't all have the same nutritional requirements. I have container plants and shrubs on the same supply line. Because container plants require so much more fertilizer than plants in the ground, I had to come up with a way to give the container plants extra feeding. My solution was to run the end of the drip tubing into a plastic film canister filled with fertilizer.

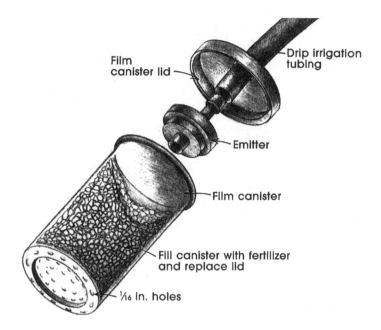

Film canister lid

Drip irrigation tubing

Emitter

Film canister

Fill canister with fertilizer and replace lid

1/16 in. holes

Modifying the film canisters is easy. First, I take the lid off the canister and drill a 1/4-in. hole in it to match the 1/4-in.-diameter tubing that carries water to my containers (the tubing is actually slightly larger than 1/4 in., so the seal between tubing and lid is tight). I remove the emitter from the end of the tubing, push the tubing through the hole and replace the emitter. I then drill several $\frac{1}{16}$-in. holes in the bottom of the canister. I fill the canister with fertilizer and snap the lid back in place (see the drawing on the facing page).

It takes about a month for the water to carry away most of the pelletized fertilizer that I use. If the plant requires more fertilizer, I just refill the film canister.

–Steve Beroldo, Berkeley, CA

Capillary watering

I've found a foolproof way to keep seedlings and moisture-loving houseplants evenly moist without the danger of overwatering. I set my containers on a nice, soft bed of capillary matting. Capillary matting is a fluffy, felt-like material that holds water like a sponge. Greenhouse growers have used it for years to bottom-water plants. The soil mix in the containers draws the moisture up from the mats through capillary action, but gravity prevents the water from saturating the soil mix, so enough oxygen remains available for root growth.

To use capillary matting, line the bottom of a shallow, waterproof pan or tray with about three layers of matting. Moisten the matting by filling the pan so that the water level is just even with the top layer of matting. Make sure that the soil mix is in contact with the matting through the drainage holes in the bottom of the container. There's no need to top water; just keep the matting moist. If you find that your mix gets too wet, allow the matting to dry out a little between waterings.

You can get capillary matting by asking your garden center to order it from a supplier or by ordering it through the mail.

–Sally Gove, Jamaica Plain, MA

Accurate watering

I've found a way to tell—often without leaving the house—when my sprinkler has put 1 in. of water on the lawn or garden. I made an oversize watering gauge, using a plastic glass, some food coloring and a patio drink holder, which is basically a cup atop a stake.

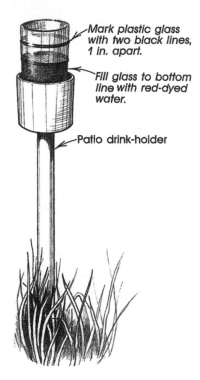

Mark plastic glass with two black lines, 1 in. apart.

Fill glass to bottom line with red-dyed water.

Patio drink-holder

I put the plastic glass in the drink holder and marked it with two $\frac{1}{4}$-in.-wide black lines, spaced 1 in. apart (see the drawing at left). You can use paint or tape to make the lines. Place them high on the glass so they clear the drink holder. Now fill the glass with water to the bottom line and add five or six drops of red food coloring to the water.

When you're ready to water, push the stake of the drink holder into the ground within range of the sprinkler. Turn on the sprinkler, and when the red water rises to the top line, you're done. Pour out an inch of water from the plastic glass (the remaining water will still be quite red), move the sprinkler and the gauge, and start again. After a few moves, you'll have to renew the food coloring.

—Caryl M. Kerber, Grosse Pointe, MI

Keeping soaker hoses in their place

I use soaker hoses that I wind through my plants to irrigate my garden. They are very efficient but difficult to work with because they don't stay put. I solved this problem by using wire insulation supports. The supports are 16 inches long and bend easily into a U shape, which I then press into the ground on both sides of the hose (see the drawing below). I place the wires about 12 inches apart.

Insulation support wires can be purchased at most building-supply stores and are priced at about $4 for a box of 100. The galvanized wire is very durable and lasts for many years.

–Ken Petersen, Franklinville, NJ

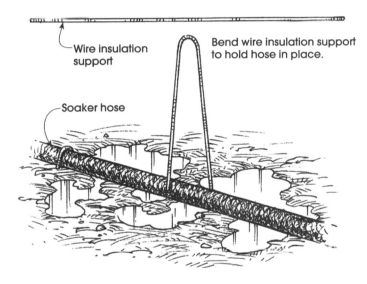

Wire insulation support

Bend wire insulation support to hold hose in place.

Soaker hose

Pest Control

Applying tweezers to Japanese beetles

I had tried everything to control Japanese beetles in my rose garden—flicking them off plants and stepping on them, dropping them into kerosene and using pheromone traps that seem only to attract more beetles. I don't like to spray pesticides to control them because pesticides ruin the roses' scent, and I'm too squeamish to crush the beetles between my fingers.

Now I carry a pair of 10-in. stainless steel tweezers on my daily stroll to admire my 45 rose bushes. I found the tweezers in a kitchen-supply catalog that advertised them for use in pulling olives or pickles out of jars. They allow me to pick off and crush offending beetles without getting poked by thorns. I leave the dead beetles around the plants in hopes that the scent will repel others.

The tweezers are also good for picking off dead or diseased leaves. They allow you to reach between stems and branches quite easily without getting poked.

—*Marian E. Leonard, Mahopac, NY*

Wired for deer

The winter before last, deer ate many of the tips of the branches on my apple trees and my plum tree. So last fall I wrapped 20-gauge galvanized bailing wire loosely around the tips of the branches, an inch out from the tip and back about 6 in. (see the drawing below). The wire shortly weathered to a dull gray and was hardly noticeable. I reasoned that biting down on a piece of wire might not be palatable for visiting deer. This spring, only two or three branches on my trees showed damage. During the winter I saw deer nibbling on the sumac bushes right next to my little orchard, so the wire treatment must have spoiled their appetite for the fruit trees.

–Harry Teder, Excelsior, MN

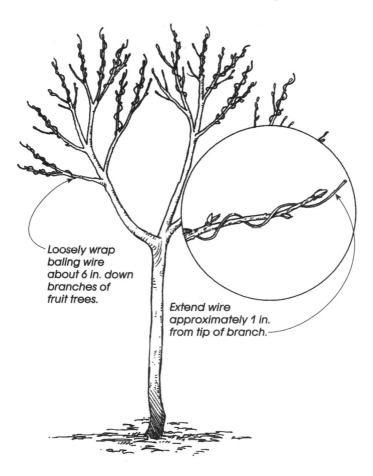

Loosely wrap baling wire about 6 in. down branches of fruit trees.

Extend wire approximately 1 in. from tip of branch.

Deer deterrent

I discovered by chance that deer dislike getting tangled in chicken wire lying loose on the ground. Over time, I scattered squares of chicken wire wherever I found deer droppings or damage in places I didn't want deer to feed. Now the deer stay in the woods or pastures and avoid the lawn and gardens.

—Vincent Wagner, West Hurley, NY

Interplanting foils deer

Here in my garden in California's hot Central Valley, flowering ground covers planted along the edges of beds are prime targets for deer. I've found that interplanting them with aromatic herbs makes them unattractive to deer. Soapwort *(Saponaria ocymoides)*, usually a favorite deer snack in my garden, is untouched when mixed with creeping thyme *(Thymus serpyllum* 'Reiter's'), and the taller dwarf plumbago *(Ceratostigma plumbaginoides)* cascades safely off a terrace in the company of prostrate rosemary *(Rosmarinus officinalis* 'Prostratus').

—Diane Cary, Winters, CA

Another deer deterrent

Deer are crackers at jumping over fences, but they don't seem to jump across them. Here on the wet side of the Cascades in rural western Washington, we have deer problems, and even elk problems. I've seen a cow elk take a 5-ft. cyclone fence from a standing start. But the hoofed marauders balk at horizontal fences. Here's how to make one.

Mow a swath around your garden, cutting the grass short, and strew it with rocks, tin cans, 2x4 blocks—whatever you have. Now lay 3-ft. or 4-ft.-wide poultry netting down (the larger 2-in. mesh is fine), leaving those little waves in it and letting the trash hold it a few inches off the ground. The idea is to make unpleasant and frightening footing for cloven feet. It's not pretty, but it works.

You can leave off the trash, but the grass grows up pretty quickly through the wire and negates the deterrent. Plan to move the wire and mow more often.

—Sandy Dengler, Ashford, WA

Corn thieves

I lost two corn plantings last year before I discovered the culprits and learned how to thwart them. Rain had delayed my first planting until the second week in June. Despite the warm weather, not a single corn sprout appeared. At the end of June, I replanted. I was beginning to think that the second batch of seeds had rotted when one morning I spotted a chipmunk in the garden. I dug around in the corn plot and sure enough, no corn kernels.

If the little scavengers wouldn't leave the kernels alone, I'd plant corn without kernels. My wife and I can only eat so much fresh corn before the rest turns tough, so I sow in small blocks—24 plants at a time. With so few plants, I could start my crop indoors. I bought peat pots, sowed two kernels in each, and set the pots under lights. A week later I set the seedlings in partial shade to harden off, and then transplanted them into the garden.

My scheme worked well, but not perfectly. To my surprise, the chipmunks rooted up a few seedlings. Apparently they could smell the remains of the kernels. That gave me another idea. I remembered reading that wild animals dislike the smell of bone meal (so do I for that matter). I mixed a little bone meal with sand to make it easier to spread and sprinkled a small handful around each plant. From then on, the crop went unmolested. Now how do I keep the little rascals out of my strawberries?

—Maurice M. Matthews, Pittsburgh, PA

Organic rabbit control

I used to lose a few 4-ft.-tall lily plants to marauding rabbits every year. Typically, the advice is to put up a 2½-ft.-high fence, but I found this aesthetically unappealing. Instead, I made a secure place for my new lily bulbs by surrounding them with shrubs. I used a mixture of *Berberis* 'Crimson Pygmy' and a low-growing variety of *Azalea* because both shrubs have dense branches that start at ground level. The maximum height of the shrubs is about 2½ ft., making them a perfect rabbit fence. Last year, I reinforced the area between the bushes with fencing. As the bushes grow together, I'll need less fence.

—Lucy Fuchs, Ambler, PA

Trapping large rodents

I have a problem with woodchucks. We have similar taste in plants, but the chucks don't just devour plants with their eyes. To get rid of these hungry herbivores, I bought a large Havahart trap, with the intention of capturing the chucks and releasing them in a remote area far from my garden. I had no problem trapping squirrels, but I couldn't catch a woodchuck, no matter what bait I used.

I noticed that many times the trap would be sprung but empty. One day I discovered why: I came home to find a woodchuck backing out of the trap. The trap's trip mechanism is in the center of the cage. A woodchuck is large enough to spring the trap without being completely inside the cage. When the door falls, it lands on his rump and does not lock.

My solution was to leave one of the trap doors shut and to set a brick on the open door. I put the bait just inside the closed door. When the woodchuck enters the trap, the weighted door comes down with greater force, spanking him on the rear end and forcing him forward, into the trap, so that the door can lock. If you find that the brick tumbles away, try wiring it to the trap door. This method doesn't always work, but I get much better results than I did without the brick.

—Susan Austin, Ipswich, MA

Rodent protection

When my clients ask me to include lilies and tulips in their landscapes, I know that precautions are in order. Several rodent species enjoy dining on the energy-rich rhizomes and bulbs of these plants. Between voles, mice and pocket gophers, what starts out as an attractive planting can soon become a ratty eyesore.

Years ago, after losing several plantings of lilies, I decided to try borrowing protection from daffodils, which rodents here don't eat. In my first experiment, I planted lilies in a bed of daffodils. The lilies went untouched. I've since found that lilies and tulips planted at normal spacings, with daffodils interplanted throughout at roughly two to four bulbs per square foot, also go untouched. The same method works for hostas, though the protection is less complete.

—Larry Loman, Wynne, AR

Pool hose protects young trees from rodents

Rabbits and rodents, such as mice and voles, love to nibble on the bark of young trees—especially in the wintertime, when other sources of food become scarce. If animals eat the bark all the way around the trunk, they can kill a tree. I protect young trees with lengths of 1½-in.-diameter plastic swimming-pool hose, the sort used to vacuum the pool (the hose is available at swimming-pool supply stores). First, using a utility knife, I cut the hose to a length equal to the distance between the ground and the first branch. Then I make a vertical

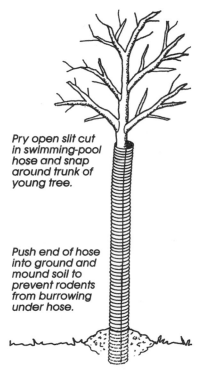

Pry open slit cut in swimming-pool hose and snap around trunk of young tree.

Push end of hose into ground and mound soil to prevent rodents from burrowing under hose.

cut the length of the hose. I pry the stiff plastic open along the slit and snap the hose around the trunk of the tree (see the drawing on the previous page). To prevent rodents from burrowing under the hose, I push the end of it an inch or so into the ground and then mound the soil up all around it.

I leave the hose in place for two or three years—until the plastic becomes brittle and begins to crack or until the trunk begins to push against the plastic. By then, the bark has become tougher and therefore much less appealing to my furry friends.

—*E.J. Biancarelli, Jessup, PA*

A raccoon fence

Raccoons are not far behind chimpanzees in reasoning power, so it's no wonder they find ways to circumvent most of the obstacles that gardeners put in their way. If these critters are stealing the fruits of your labor, try assembling my simple and inexpensive fence. For over 15 years it has kept raccoons out of my garden without a single failure. It seems to foil woodchucks, too.

My raccoon fence is just a 36-in.-wide strip of six-mil black plastic (black plastic doesn't deteriorate from sunlight as quickly as clear plastic does) stapled to pressure-treated 2x2 stakes. The raccoons can't jump the plastic. Nor can they climb it; their claws slip. And since raccoons won't dig unless trapped, the fence completely befuddles them.

Putting up the fence is easy. First measure the area you want to enclose, and then purchase the appropriate quantities of materials from the lumberyard or the hardware store. Cut the 2x2s to make 3-ft.- to 4-ft.-long stakes. Pound the stakes into the ground at 10-ft. intervals to a height of about 30 in. Next, staple or tack the plastic to the outside of the stakes so that the bottom 3 in. to 6 in. of the plastic rests on the ground. Where sections of plastic meet, be sure that they overlap so that the rascals can't sneak through. If you already have a fence around your garden, simply clip the plastic to the fence with clothespins.

Now you can plant your corn or whatever it is that tempts these voracious animals and know that it will be waiting for you when the time comes to harvest.

—*Alton Eliason, Northford, CT*

Hot peppers keep squirrels from digging bulbs

Squirrels seem to have a nose for freshly turned soil. In my neighborhood, they often unearth spring-blooming bulbs and devour them within hours after they've been planted. To keep squirrels at bay, I sprinkle powdered hot red peppers (crushed peppers will probably work just as well) liberally over newly planted beds. The peppers repel the squirrels long enough for a soaking rain to dissipate the odor of fresh earth.

Buy powdered peppers in bulk from an ethnic market. The small tins or bottles in the spice department of the grocery store are too pricey for garden use.

–Diane Sutliff, Chicago, Il.

Cat-proofing

A landscaping client who hung birdhouses in a pine tree asked if I could protect the nests from climbing cats. I came up with the cat guard shown below. It keeps cats from climbing the tree, but lets squirrels freely pass up and down the trunk.

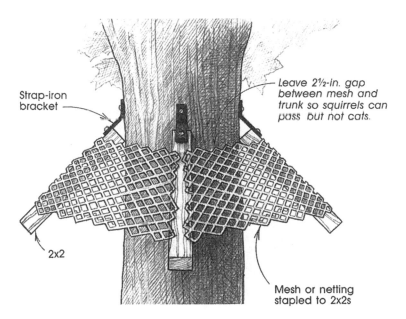

Strap-iron bracket

Leave 2½-in. gap between mesh and trunk so squirrels can pass but not cats.

2x2

Mesh or netting stapled to 2x2s

The cat guard is a conelike collar of plastic mesh stapled to 2x2s. I cut the mesh from the bottom of old nursery flats, but you could use netting. Leave a 2½-in. gap between the mesh and the trunk of the tree so squirrels can pass. Fasten the 2x2s to the trunk with screws and metal brackets bent at a 135° angle. You can back out the screws a little every year or two to keep them from being overgrown as the tree adds girth.

–Amos J. Jones, Seattle, WA

Net keeps bunnies at bay

I like to grow perennials from seed, but I've found out that these small plants are a favorite lunch for hungry rabbits. My effective, no-cost solution is to use plastic mesh produce bags (the kind that onions come in) to cover and protect the young plants.

Mesh produce bag

Stake

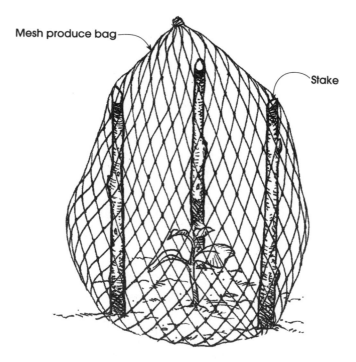

I push three or four small wooden stakes or twigs into the soil around the plants (see the drawing on the facing page). Then I slip the produce bag over the stakes to hold the bag upright. The rabbits do not chew through the plastic, and the plants are protected while getting light and air.

–Dorris Olson, Duluth, MN

Cat fur scares rabbits away

Last year I noticed that many of my perennials and annuals were eaten—buds chewed off, plants gnawed to the ground. I assumed it was some kind of rodent since there are no deer in my area. I tried several commercial remedies to no avail.

One morning I spotted the culprit: a rabbit. Realizing that the cat is the rabbit's natural enemy, I decided to put my house cat to use. Since I didn't want to harm the rabbit—only chase him away—I collected the fur from my cat's daily brushing. I placed it around my garden, especially by plants that the rabbit preferred. Within days the rabbit was gone. I continued to replace the cat fur after every rain that year, and the rabbit never returned.

–Eileen DeNezza, South Orange, NJ

Newspaper prevents spread of pests

To keep my indoor garden work area neat, I cover the table with several sheets of fully unfolded newspaper. After I finish transplanting seedlings or working with a houseplant, I lift the corners of the top sheet of newspaper (carefully wrapping up spilled potting soil, dead leaves and other debris), and put it aside to add to the compost heap. This practice leaves a clean sheet ready for the next plant and reduces the chance of spreading undetected pests or diseases. When I get down to the last sheet of newspaper, I spread out several more layers.

–Ethel Fried, West Hartford, CT

Vole patrol

Long before I learned that voles even existed, these small rodents wiped out 100 ginseng roots I planted. The voles had moved on to my blueberry patch and killed off five bushes before I stumbled upon a way to stop them—a mixed terrier puppy. Although I knew that terriers were good rodent hunters, it was my then-7-year-old son who chose her; it was a case of puppy love.

When we brought her home from the pound, she dug and dug. There were holes everywhere and dead voles strewn about the yard, but after two or three months, she had wiped them out and quit digging. We filled in the holes, remulched the berry bushes and have not had a problem with voles, or holes, since. That was five years ago.

–Dorothy Lee, Leicester, NC

Gophers and young trees

Gophers like to burrow in gardens here, and can cause serious damage to newly transplanted young trees by disturbing their anchorage, breaking roots and opening air pockets that dry out roots. When I set out a new tree, I line the planting hole with chicken wire so that the tree gets a chance to settle in and grow without disruption. Chicken wire will rust and eventually break. Meanwhile, the roots can grow through the mesh.

–Charles Estep, Sr., Riverside, CA

Blueberry netting

When I first planted my blueberries a few years ago, I resisted using netting because of the way it looked and the work and expense involved. However, as the plants began to bear fruit, the need for netting became apparent.

I decided to create my own framework for netting that was unobtrusive, inexpensive and easy to set up. I wanted to use it only during the fruiting season, and I wanted to be able to store it easily during the rest of the year.

My solution was purchased bird netting, 8-ft. lengths of ⅜-in. rebar poles embedded around the perimeter of the blueberry patch,

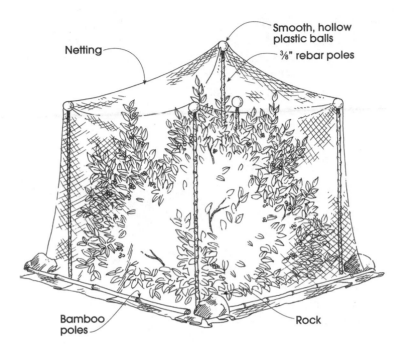

Netting

Smooth, hollow plastic balls

⅜" rebar poles

Bamboo poles

Rock

and one 9-ft. length in the center. On top of each pole, I slipped a 3-in.-diameter, hollow, plastic ball in which I had made a hole. The balls allow the netting, which I place over them, to be moved easily for positioning. I anchor the net by laying bamboo poles over the edges and filling the gaps at the corners with flat rocks (see the drawing above).

—*Sue Custance, Athens, GA*

Squirrel-proof feeder

I like to attract birds to my garden, but squirrels get in the way. They had no trouble burglarizing the bird feeders I hung from trees and my house, and the only place for a post-top feeder they couldn't vault aboard was the patio, where a post would be a nuisance in summer. So I designed a removable post, and for good measure I added a baffle to keep squirrels from shinnying up it.

I bought a 2-ft. length of galvanized pipe that the feeder post fit snugly inside, dug a hole and dropped the pipe in. I made sure the pipe was vertical and fixed it solidly in place by surrounding it with concrete. Then I covered the mouth with a rubber bathtub plug to keep out dirt. In fall I pull the plug and slip the pole in, where it stands upright and secure, and in spring I pull the pole and replace the plug.

To foil climbing squirrels, I modified a large juice can and hung it under the feeder. I cut out the top and bottom lids of the can, slipped it over the pole and wired it underneath the feeder. An upwardly mobile squirrel can't wrap its arms around the can or get a grip on it. If the squirrel stays on the pole, it ends up inside the can.

–*Caryl M. Kerber, Grosse Pointe Park, MI*

Bird-proof fruit

We planted three blueberry bushes for a "decorative fruiting hedge," as the catalog put it, but soon discovered the conflict between "decorative" and "fruiting." To fend off the birds, we had to swathe the plants in netting, held away from the fruit by improvised posts. Not too "decorative."

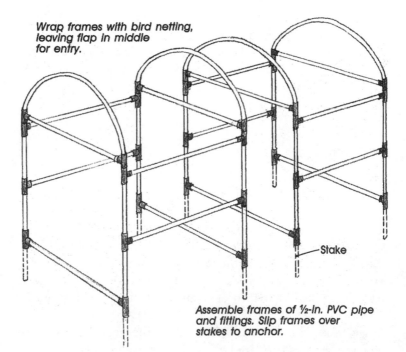

Wrap frames with bird netting, leaving flap in middle for entry.

—Stake

Assemble frames of ½-in. PVC pipe and fittings. Slip frames over stakes to anchor.

So, we set out to make a more elegant structure and soon found the ideal materials: ½-in. PVC plastic pipe and fittings. Light and inexpensive, they're as easy to assemble as Tinkertoys. The pipe's flexibility suggested a crowning touch: arches.

As the drawing on the facing page shows, we made a tunnellike PVC frame with two pairs of arches and crossbraces for stability. Each pair of arches is 4 ft. square and about 7 ft. tall. We anchored the arches with plastic-covered metal garden stakes, driven deep into the ground and extending well up into the legs. Instead of gluing the pipe and fittings with PVC cement, we assembled them dry. The joints hold tight, and we can easily dismantle, store and reassemble the frame, if need be. All the materials came to $20.

When berries appear, I cover the frame with plastic bird netting (available in several sizes from Gardener's Supply, 128 Intervale Rd., Burlington, VT 05401). You have to fit the pieces to your frame. I wrap one length around the ends and sides, and sew it with string to the netting over the arches. I leave a flap for a door on one side, between the two pairs of arches.

—Ann Cummings, Adamsville, RI

Slugging it out: Minimizing hosta damage

I have a hosta bed in dense shade under two huge hemlocks. The soil is very dry there, despite the addition of quantities of peat moss and humus. I used to mulch the hostas with cedar bark to reduce evaporation and retain soil moisture, but the slugs ate everything. One year I neglected to put down the mulch and discovered there was much less slug damage. I no longer use mulch, but I do water heavily early in the morning. By nighttime the surface moisture has evaporated and the slugs avoid the dry soil.

Since I began this, there have been fewer and fewer slugs each year and the appearance of the hosta has improved tremendously.

—Diane Campbell, New Milford, CT

Chicken-wire row covers for strawberries

We've come up with a way to keep the robins away from our strawberry crop. We designed row covers with walls of chicken wire instead of plastic, and our son John built them.

The covers are easy to put together with materials available at hardware and building-supply stores. With a hacksaw, John cut square electrical conduit pipe (round will work equally well) into 48-in. lengths. Using a vice, he bent each piece of pipe in the middle to form a 60° angle. (A 90° angle will work, too). Next, he cut 10-ft. lengths of 1x4 lumber (adjust the length to suit your needs) and painted them to protect them from the elements.

Each cover has three conduit supports, one at each end and one in the middle, and three 1x4s, two connecting the ends of the conduit pieces and one (for additional support) at the apex (see the photo below). John fastened the wood to the supports with metal tapping screws turned into pre-drilled holes. He covered the frame with 4-ft.-wide chicken wire, which he cut 3 ft. longer than the frame. He used the extra 18 in. of wire on each end to fold

over the ends or to overlap with neighboring row covers. He attached the wire to the frame with staples.

When we need to get at the strawberries for weeding or harvesting, we simply tip the covers over on their sides. At season's end, we stack them in a corner of the garden.

—Francis and Betty Flynn, Billings, MT

An eggshell barrier

Our acre here in central Vermont appears to be a haven for slugs. It has been difficult to endure watching a favorite plant be destroyed by the soft-bodied creatures. But during the last two years, I've had a marked decrease in slug activity.

The reason is because I have been scattering crushed eggshells around individual plants and along the edges of flower beds. When the slugs attempt to crawl through the shells, the rough edges scratch or cut their bodies, forcing them to retreat.

Every cook in our home who uses eggs in a recipe saves the shells, rinses them out and places them to dry on a plate. The process takes but a minute. We store the dried, crushed eggshells in a large container and sprinkle them in the garden when needed.

A totally unexpected benefit is that the crushed eggshells seem to attract birds. Tree swallows swoop in for a snack and robins pick up a piece and fly away with it. House finches arrive in a noisy family group for a picnic. This is one delightful benefit I didn't anticipate when I began this experiment.

—Lucretia R. Richie, Randolph, VT

"Dry cleaning" aphids

Annoyed by aphids but faced with strict water-conservation measures, I've found an alternative to spraying the pests off my plants with a hose. I use a baby's hairbrush or the handle-less head of an old nylon broom to brush the beasts off tender shoots and tendrils. The hairbrush and nylon broom have soft, dense bristles that are gentler to the plants and more effective at removing aphids than my fingertips.

—Trish Kaspar, San Jose, CA

Keeping snails out of trees

You can never have too many tips to keep snails at bay. Here's what we use to keep snails out of citrus trees in southern California.

To keep snails from climbing into the trees, I wrap a 6-in.-wide band of copper foil or thin copper roof flashing around the trunk 6 to 8 in. off the ground (see the drawing below). When the snail's moist body touches the copper, it receives a mild shock. The snail then backs away, somewhat stunned, and will stay put until it is hand-picked from the trunk.

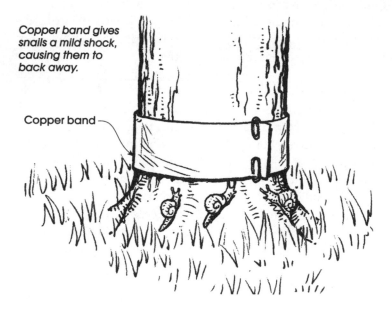

Copper band gives snails a mild shock, causing them to back away.

Copper band

I cut the copper band one-and-one-half the circumference of the tree to allow room for the trunk to expand as it grows. I use one tack or staple to fasten the copper to the tree. Then I wrap the band tightly around the tree with the ends overlapping, fastening the ends with large copper paper clips. The clips allow the band to expand as the tree grows.

—Daryl Turner, Fallbrook, CA

Nontoxic wasp control

My family once lived in an English village where wasps followed us around and were nasty. One of our neighbors said we could rid ourselves of the wasps that nested around the house if we put 3 in. of malt vinegar in a beer bottle and put the bottle outside the kitchen door. We thought the advice was crazy, but it worked—and it works for me still, here in California. The wasps evidently love the smell of vinegar, crawl into the narrow neck of the bottle, hit the fumes, fall in and drown. You don't need malt vinegar. I use white vinegar, or whatever I have, and it's just as effective.

—Jackie Bristow, Sacramento, CA

Morning slug patrol

Each morning I go on slug patrol with a sharp shovel in hand. When I meet a slug on his way to breakfast, I use the shovel to cut him in half and I leave the remains to attract his relatives. I use the same method in the evening, and after about two weeks, no more slugs for a while.

Other things that seem to help control slugs in my garden are diatomaceous earth (a nontoxic mineral product made from the fossilized shells of an algae and available at garden centers), growing vegetables in raised beds with gravel in between, and composting along the outer edges of the garden with straw and/or seaweed.

—Claire Hellar, Waldron, WA

Slow down slugs with pine needles

The Pacific Northwest is slug heaven. The slimy rascals love our cool climate. Overnight they can devour entire leaves and turn others to lace. Primroses are among their favorite foods, so I was surprised one year to note that primroses in a bed I had mulched with pine needles suffered very little slug damage. I can't say that pine needles will deter slugs in every situation, but it's worth a try. If you've got a friend with a big pine tree, the experiment will cost you nothing more than your labor.

—Janet Wartinger, Seattle, WA

Trap slugs with flower pots

Here is a safe, simple way to trap slugs in the garden. Take two clay flower pots of different sizes—a 4-in. pot and a 6-in. pot, for example—and soak them in a tub of water (new pots should be soaked for about 48 hours). Then place them upside down with the smaller one inside the larger one in a shady location near plants that show evidence of slug damage. Keep the pots moist. After three or four days, lift the top pot and you will find slugs sleeping in the little "house" you have provided for them (see the drawing below). Scrape the slugs into a disposable container with a tight-fitting lid and toss it into the trash.

Since slugs eat at night and sleep in the daytime, check and empty pots in the middle of the day. Make your daylight rounds a couple of times a week, and before long your slug problem will be solved.

—Gail Hogue, Pascagoula, MS

Large clay pot

Slugs

Small clay pot

Nest a small, moistened clay pot inside a large one. Lift large pot at mid-day to find slugs sleeping inside.

Nettle tea controls aphids

I have had good results using nettle "tea" in my greenhouse to get rid of aphids. I grow my own nettles just to control these pests. Dried nettle that is sold in health-food stores is equally effective, but for the amount I need, it can get expensive. Because the nettle leaves (Cnidoscolus) are so prickly, I wear a heavy rubber glove on my left hand as I clip the leaves with my right.

To make the tea, the leaves must rot, not just brew. I fill two-thirds of a 5-gal. bucket with nettle leaves. The leaves will disintegrate faster if they are chopped into 1-in. pieces. Then I add luke-warm water to fill the bucket. I arrived at the temperature by trial and error—boiling water will scald the leaves and not allow them to rot; cold water won't allow the leaves to disintegrate. After adding the water, I stir the mixture every day until the leaves no longer float to the top. Then I let it sit for a week or two, stirring occasionally or covering the bucket if the brew starts to smell bad. You'll know the tea is ready when it smells terrible.

The tea will be very strong when it's finished and should be diluted. I add 1 cup nettle tea to 1 gal. water, then water plants at their base, repeating in a month if necessary. I usually make more than one batch since a second dose is often needed to kill all of the aphids.

Hint: To eliminate the most aphids, spray plants with a hose to knock aphids off leaves, then water with the tea.

This brew also nourishes the plants. Comfrey tea made the same way is also an excellent organic fertilizer.

—Shoshanna Schwimmer, Renick, WV

Safe bug lure

I like blackberries, but so do June beetles—$1\frac{1}{2}$-in.-long, metallic-green, industrial-strength fruit chewers. By mid-July, my five thornless blackberry bushes are weighted down with berries and pesky hordes of June beetles. The beetles infest my bushes so heavily that they intimidate even the most determined berry picker.

Since I'm reluctant to spray insecticides, it took time to find a remedy. By accident, I discovered how to lure and trap June beetles with the smell of fruit. Now I place several 5-gal. buckets half-filled with soapy water within 10 ft. of the bushes, and add a rotten peach or some damaged blackberries to the water for a lure. The beetles fly in and drown. The smell of fruit also attracts toads, so if you use other containers, make sure they're at least 10 in. tall. Otherwise the toads will hop in and drown.

Despite my aromatic buckets, I still find a few beetles on the blackberry bushes, but I catch them easily with a variation of the bucket trap: I hold a bowl of soapy water under a berry cluster and rap the cluster sharply with one finger. The beetles fall into the bowl and drown.

–Jan Fergus, Hatwood, MD

Pouring boiling water on the problem

As unusual as it seems, my 6-qt. kettle is one of my most helpful gardening aids. When I want to control weeds and other unwanted plant volunteers around my property, I use boiling water from my kettle to stop them. I simply pour boiling water over these vexatious plants, and soon they die, without my having to reach for harmful pesticides. This procedure is especially useful when tackling weeds and grasses growing along my neighbor's fence, in sidewalk cracks and in other hard-to-reach places.

I found another application for this cure last summer when I tried to remove the roots of an established shrub that was growing close to the sidewalk. No matter how much I cut down or dug up, the shrub kept sending up new growth. Finally, I poured boiling water over it four times in one day. The next day I was able to remove the stump and all traces of the shrub.

–Claire Moshil, Chicago, IL

Earwig traps

Earwigs are a serious and persistent problem in our arid summer climate here in northern California. Seedlings disappear overnight, and flowers and berries are spoiled. Although a floating row cover can provide some protection, the soil used to cover the edges of the material reduces the life span of the cover. I've tried spraying with insecticidal soap after nightfall, but found another option in my kitchen pantry.

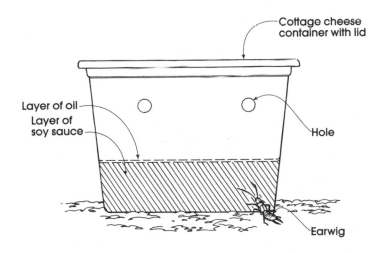

Cottage cheese container with lid

Layer of oil
Layer of soy sauce

Hole

Earwig

I simply pour about an inch of soy sauce into a can or plastic container, and top it with a film of vegetable oil (see the illustration above). I then put the container in the garden to attract and drown earwigs.

Cottage cheese or sour cream containers work well. I punch two holes in their sides near the top and replace the lid to reduce evaporation. Once a week, I discard the solution and put out a fresh container.

–Marianne G. Michener, Petaluma, CA

The color yellow attracts fungus gnats

Last year I had an unusually large number of fungus gnats crawling over and flying around the houseplants and seedlings I grow under fluorescent lights in my basement. Fungus gnats are tiny flies that, as their name suggests, feed on decaying organic matter and on the fungi that break down organic matter. According to pest books, most fungus gnats don't harm plants, but I still didn't want them flying around my basement and finding their way upstairs. I'd read that some insects are attracted to the color yellow, so, as an experiment, I placed yellow plastic bowls filled with water among my plants. Within a week hundreds of fungus gnats were floating in the water, and the infestation came to an end.

—Rosemary Pichler, St. Louis, MO

Homemade traps for whiteflies

Here's an economical way to control whiteflies, which can be serious pests of plants grown indoors—in the house or the greenhouse. Whiteflies congregate in huge numbers under leaves and suck the sap. The easiest and safest way to kill them is to set out yellow cards covered with a sticky substance (whiteflies are drawn to the yellow color). You can buy traps through catalogs or from garden centers, but I prefer to make my own. The sticky substance on commercial traps dries out quickly, and when the trap dries up or gets covered with bugs, you have to throw it out.

I make reusable traps out of window glass (I use old panes of greenhouse glass, but any clear glass will do). I spray one side of the glass with bright yellow paint. After the paint dries, I spread a very thin coat of motor oil on the other side. Then I set the piece of glass, oil side up, near infested plants. The whiteflies go for the yellow color and get stuck in the oil. Every month or so, I wipe the glass clean and apply a fresh coat of oil.

—Paul E. Reiffeiss, Stanfordville, NY

A sticky solution to rose-cane borers

The larvae of several insects will burrow down the center of a rose cane. These borers can do a fair amount of damage and are difficult to control with pesticides. I have found that the best way to deal with these troublesome larvae is to exclude them. To do this, I seal the tip of each cane after pruning with a drop of nontoxic white glue (see the drawing at right). The glue dries relatively clear and is impenetrable to invaders. This is an easy and environmentally kind solution to rose-cane borers.

–Robert H. Nelson, Seattle, WA

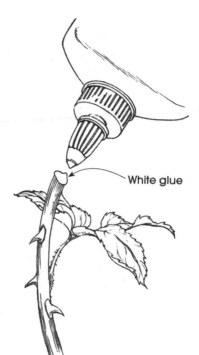

White glue

Tenderizer for insect bites

Last summer a dermatologist friend of mine, who also has a background in pharmacology, told me that meat tenderizers containing papain, an enzyme derived from papaya, can alleviate the pain and itching of insect bites. Not too long after our conversation, I unfortunately had a chance to test his assertion.

While grooming my window boxes one morning, I was stung in the palm of my hand by a tiny yellow jacket. The pain was excruciating. As my friend suggested, I ran inside (it's important to treat the bite immediately) and applied Adolph's meat tenderizer—the one without garlic and herb flavoring—to the wound by wetting the skin and sprinkling a small amount of the granular powder on it. By the next day, you couldn't even see where I had been bitten. Now I carry a bottle of tenderizer in my bucket when I work outdoors, and I also bring bottles to all my gardening friends.

–Phyllis Finkelstein, Scarsdale, NY

Midas touch in reverse

Sometimes weeds in my garden will grow in between or too close to treasured plants to safely spray with weed killer (for example, blackberries growing up through hosta). To overcome this problem, I put on a pair of rubber gloves, and over the rubber gloves, I put on a pair of cotton gloves. The rubber gloves protect my hands from the herbicide, while the cotton gloves hold in the herbicide and act as an applicator. I dip my fingertips into a solution of liquid herbicide, and anything I wipe dies (see the drawing below). Sort of a reverse King Midas touch!

—Eddie Rhoades, Austell, GA

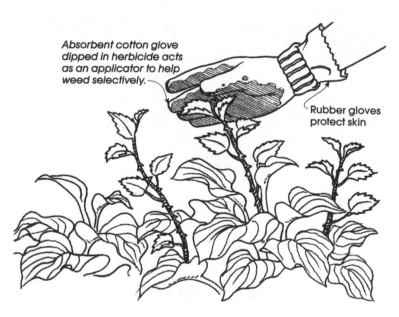

Absorbent cotton glove dipped in herbicide acts as an applicator to help weed selectively.

Rubber gloves protect skin

Eight-legged insecticides

House spiders make quick work of houseplant pests. Whenever I find a spider, I pick it up carefully with a tissue and take it to a group of my houseplants. Spiders have no interest in me, but they love to feed on the insects and other pests that plague plants. I think they work just as well as chemical sprays. When the spiders move along, you can be sure your plants are pest-free.

—Joyce Descloux, Randolph, NJ

Dishwashing soap controls powdery mildew

Last year we received three times the average rainfall in our area of southwestern Texas. One of the consequences of all that rain was an epidemic of powdery mildew. The older, thicker euonymus hedges, including one along one side of our property, seemed to be the hardest hit. In a Master Gardener class, my husband and I had learned about the experimental use of dishwashing detergent as an alternative to traditional fungicides, so my husband, with the co-operation of our neighbor, decided to try an experiment of his own on our hedge. My husband sprayed our side of the hedge with Dawn dishwashing liquid; our neighbor sprayed his side with a fungicide recommended for use against powdery mildew. The side sprayed with Dawn cleared up faster and stayed free of disease just as long (about three weeks) as the side sprayed with fungicide—at a fraction of the cost.

If you have a problem with powdery mildew, try dishwashing liquid as a remedy. My husband used four tablespoons in a hose-end sprayer, which works out to about a teaspoon per gallon of water, and sprayed every morning until the signs of the disease were gone. We heard Dawn was effective, so we used it; other brands may also thwart mildew.

—Jane Martin, Monahans, TX

Carrot flies

In trials that I repeated for several years, I found that growing common sage and carrots together deterred carrot flies, whose larvae feed on carrot roots. My garden was laid out in 4-ft.-wide raised beds, oriented east-west. In some plots, I planted the carrots in rows across the beds, leaving 1 ft. free on the north side for the sage (so the sage plants would not shade the carrots). In other plots, I planted carrots alone. Every year, the carrots growing alone showed far more damage than did the carrots growing with sage.

—Ellen Jantzen, St. Louis, MO

Homemade fungal control

I am always looking for ideas to fight plant disease without harming my surroundings. Last spring I got an idea while I was washing my hands.

I was using the kind of antibacterial hand soap that comes in a pump dispenser and is sold in supermarkets. It reminded me of the trick of spraying kitchen soap mixed with water onto plants to control spider mites. I decided to try it on my wild rose, which suffers every spring from gray mold. I mixed six or seven squirts of antibacterial soap with water in my standard 1-qt. hand sprayer and doused my rose. It halted the mold in its tracks.

Since then, I have sprayed this brew on a photinia shrub suffering from black spot, on asters, other roses and a honeysuckle vine suffering from rust. The soap solution took care of all of these ailments and saved me a bundle on fungicides.

To be careful, I would recommend experimenting and spraying a little on a couple of leaves before dousing an entire plant.

–Stephen Phillips, Greenville, SC

Salad oil fungicide for houseplants

A friend once told me that I could give a shiny appearance to the leaves of my houseplants by wiping them with salad oil. It occurred to me some time later, as I looked at a recently purchased rex begonia that had come down with a bad case of fungus, that the salad oil might also have a therapeutic use. I removed all the badly infected leaves, then swabbed oil on the remaining affected leaves with a Q-tip. I did this almost daily, watching for the appearance of fungus spots on newly opened leaves, until the disease went away. Today the plant is a picture of health.

I can't say why this worked. My theory is that the oil prevents the fungus from launching its spores into the air. I have also heard that the oil may be capable of suffocating the fungus without harming the plant. Whatever the reason, it worked for me. If you have a houseplant that is so infected that you are ready to throw it out, you might give this treatment a try first.

–Frances Neil, Dobbs Ferry, NY

Removing scale insects from houseplants

I've discovered an effective way of removing fluffy, soft scale insects from my orchids and other houseplants. I use Buf-Puf facial cleansing sponges (the kind that don't have soap in them) moistened with isopropyl alcohol to gently scrub the insects away. The sponges, which are made by 3M and are available in the cosmetics section of drugstores, have a surface that is rough enough to do the job but not rough enough to hurt the plant. In my experience, Buf-Puf sponges work better than cotton swabs, which are too soft, and toothbrushes, which are too large to reach into small crevices. As effective as these sponges are, one scrubbing usually is not enough. I always check back once a week for two or three weeks to make certain that I've put an end to the infestation.

—*Georgian Franczyk, Brighton, MI*

Lizards in the solarium

I have a small (7- by 10-ft.) solarium adjacent to my kitchen. Since I have no door between the kitchen and solarium, I wanted biological insect control. Predatory wasps were obviously out, as were sprays of any kind.

My solution was a gecko—a small, harmless, tropical, insectivorous lizard. I purchased one at a pet store and let the critter loose in the solarium. It immediately disappeared, but a few days later I saw it sunning itself on the windowsill. The insect problem lessened considerably over the next few months. Since the solarium gets down to 50°F on winter nights, I bought a warming rock from the pet store to keep the gecko comfortable. I had no problem with lizard droppings, and my working pet needed no water or food as long as the insect supply was adequate. I think this solution would work equally well in a greenhouse.

—*Theresa Overfield, Salt Lake City, UT*

Controlling houseplant pests

A dental hygiene water jet is perfect for dislodging the spider mites, aphids and other insects that breed on my houseplants in the low humidity of the winter heating season. The water jet's narrow, forceful stream of water gets into every nook and cranny of the plants.

I set the insect-infested plant into my empty bathtub where I can freely spray water without damaging the surroundings. I fill the water jet with lukewarm water and a dash of dish detergent, which helps clean the plant. I direct the jet of water at the upper and lower surface of every leaf and leaf node, adjusting the force to suit the plant—for plants with delicate leaves, I set the jet on low, while for plants with sturdier leaves, I raise the setting.

The results depend on the infestation. On some plants, one spraying entirely eliminates the pests. On others, regular spraying keeps them in check, without eradicating them entirely.

—Pat Taylor, Washington, DC

Weed barriers

I use landscaping fabric for weed control around shrubs, trees and large perennials. It allows water to go through but not sunlight, and works well as a weed barrier. It's unattractive stuff, though, and I don't want it showing in the garden. After a bit of experimenting, I've learned how to hide it nicely with mulch.

When I first tried mulch atop the fabric, I had a problem with birds scratching in the mulch and lifting the fabric. Mulch, light and ultimately weeds got underneath.

Now I anchor the cloth with pins made from coat-hanger wire cut into 10-in. lengths, with the top inch or so bent at a right angle to make a head. I push the pins through the fabric into the ground and they help keep the fabric in place.

For mulch, I first spread a layer of fine material, such as pine needles, then top it with heavier, coarser material, such as bark chips. The fabric seems less likely to show through two-step mulch.

—Martha Byrd, Davidson, NC

Weed-collecting stations

I can't help myself. When I walk around my garden and see a weed, I just have to pull it. Inevitably, before I finish my tour, I end up with a handful of weeds. Where to toss them? Dashing to the compost pile requires a big detour. Dropping them on the ground to await a return trip is unsightly.

In a friend's garden, I came upon a solution. At strategic points along the fence that surrounds his garden, he hangs bushel baskets on hooks to serve as weed-collecting stations. On walks through the garden, he drops weeds into the baskets as he passes by. Bushel baskets are lightweight and unobtrusive, and they allow water to drain out the bottom, avoiding the creation of a distasteful weed soup. When the baskets are full, he empties them into a wheelbarrow or garden cart.

Last summer, I borrowed my friend's tip. I couldn't find bushel baskets, so I bought brown plastic pails and drilled several holes in the bottoms. The time spent sinking a few posts and hanging a few pails was quickly made up manyfold.

—Sydney Eddison, Newtown, CT

Bag-a-weed

I've come up with a way to pull up rash-inducing weeds such as poison ivy without touching the plant. I put my arm into one of the long bags that the newspaper comes in on rainy days. I pull the weed with my plastic-sheathed hand; then, with my other hand, I pull the plastic down my arm and over the plant. Both weed and plastic bag go into the trash. This same technique is also useful for pulling weeds that tend to scatter their seeds.

—Mrs. Robert Lauderdale, Lexington, KY

Attracting Birds

Leftover yarn helps birds build nests
During fall and winter, I collect loose threads from my sewing and snippets of yarn from my knitting and wind them into very loose balls. In the spring, when the birds are arguing over nesting territories, I hook the wads of thread and yarn on twigs in the trees that surround my garden. When nest building gets under way, the birds find a convenient source of fiber close at hand. They seem to prefer natural fibers, so I use only cotton and wool. The trees on our land yield bumper crops of chicks in nests laced with my sewing leftovers, and my garden gets lots of attention from the hard-working, insect-eating parents.

—Betsy P. Race, Euclid, OH

Birds in a basket
The Carolina wrens that frequent my garden often build nests in dangerous (accessible to cats) locations. To help out the birds, three years ago I nailed a picture hook that I had pulled open with

Mail basket

Picture hook

pliers on a wall in my carport. On that I hung the kind of basket designed to hold mail (see the drawing above). High on the wall, the basket is protected from rain, wind and cats. The soft wool I added for nesting material must have been inviting, because occupancy was almost immediate.

Each season wrens (the same pair, perhaps?) have successfully raised their family in that basket. It has been rewarding for me to watch the busy parents respond to increasingly louder cheeps, and eventually see the basket shake as the nestlings grow more vigorous before becoming fledglings and flying away.

—*Barbara L. Ruff, Athens, GA*

Dripping water attracts birds

I learned this trick for attracting birds to the garden from my mother. I don't know where she got it, but she's been doing it for years, and it's just astounding how well it works.

I make a hole in a plastic milk jug, fill the jug with water, hang it from a tree and put a clay or plastic saucer underneath. The water drips very slowly into the saucer, kerplunk, kerplunk. The state ornithologist told me that birds can hear that sound a long way off. I raise the saucer on bricks because a lot of birds are not comfortable on the ground. I'm sure a birdbath would do just as well in place of the saucer. I paint the milk jug green to make it less noticeable in the tree, but I imagine you could find a more attractive reservoir.

You want a drop every eight to ten seconds, so you have to make the smallest hole possible in the milk jug. I use a sewing needle and barely push the tip through the plastic. It's tricky—you might need to practice on two or three jugs to get it right. I don't know why a slow drip works better than a fast drip, but it does. It's also more convenient: At eight to ten seconds between drops, a milk jug takes about two days to empty.

—Felder Rushing, Jackson, MS

A birdbath for all wildlife

Birds aren't the only visitors to my birdbath. Four-legged friends such as raccoons and skunks from the neighboring county park often stop by at night for a drink. I knew that I had had nocturnal visitors when I'd find the concrete birdbath bowl knocked off its pedestal and lying on the ground—sometimes broken into several pieces. After replacing the bowl several times, I hit on the idea of inverting the base of the birdbath. I dug a hole about 18 inches deep and set the narrow end (the "top") of the base into the hole. I then packed the soil around the base (see the drawing on the facing page). For additional stability, I filled the open end with soil. My new and improved birdbath works beautifully. The larger

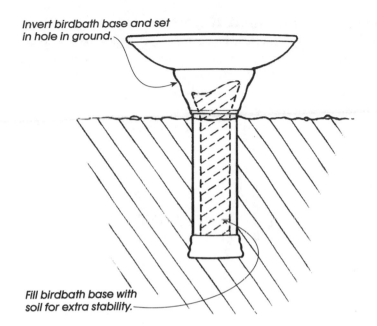

Invert birdbath base and set in hole in ground.

Fill birdbath base with soil for extra stability.

diameter of the base "bottom" provides better support for the bowl, and the reduced height makes it more convenient for my furry guests to reach the water.

—Joan Johnson, Cincinnati, OH

Brush piles for birds

Birds love brush piles. We found out about their fondness for brush quite by accident after we moved into our new house last fall. We were scurrying about getting our yard ready for winter, so when our son pruned some dead branches and piled them high in a corner of the yard, they just sat there until spring. Birds of all sorts enjoyed that complex of perches all winter long. And the cats steered clear of the prickly pile. When fall arrives this year, I'm going to leave a stack of dead, dry limbs and brush in a corner of the yard again—on purpose.

—L.W. Bergeron, Halfway, OR

Another dripping bird waterer

Birds can be very beneficial to a garden as they devour insects and weed seeds. In addition, their perky presence is always a source of joy to the gardener. Bird waterers are a great way to attract these feathered friends, but many birds, especially during migration, will pass right by if they don't hear the sound of splashing water. To fix this problem, my husband and I suspended a pottery birdbath

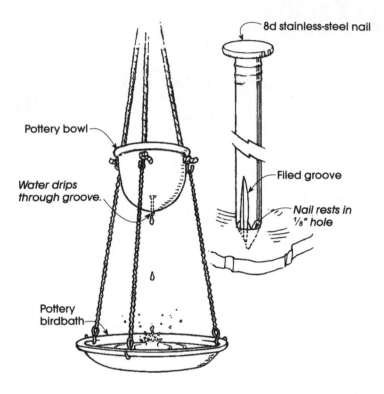

8d stainless-steel nail

Pottery bowl

Water drips through groove.

Filed groove

Nail rests in ⅛" hole

Pottery birdbath

via S-hooks and chain from a pottery bowl (that was sold as a hanging planter), which we hung from a tree branch. We carefully drilled an ⅛-in. hole in the bottom of the bowl and filed a groove in an 8d stainless-steel nail, which is inserted into the hole to regulate the drip (see the drawing above). The bowl is filled, and the slow, steady splash acts as a signpost, letting all our airborne buddies know where they can get a sip of fresh water.

–Judy Megan, Woodbury, CT

Handmade, squirrel-proof bird feeder

I have designed a special bird feeder to make life more comfortable for the many birds that share my garden. I cut out one side of a 3-liter plastic soda bottle and used two wooden dowels to form perches for the birds. The top perch is a resting spot; the bottom perch gives birds access to the seed.

I've also made a round roof from sheet metal to keep the bird food dry. I used tin snips to cut a 1-ft. circle of sheet metal, and snipped a hole in the center of the circle. I made a cut from the outside edge to the center hole, folded the sides over to form a cone, and fastened it with a sheet-metal screw (see the illustration below). The squirrels can't get a foothold on the metal roof, and the plastic bottle is too flimsy to support their weight. This roof can be used either on the soda-bottle feeder or on the store-bought tubular plastic feeders.

–Donald Schmucker, Derry, PA

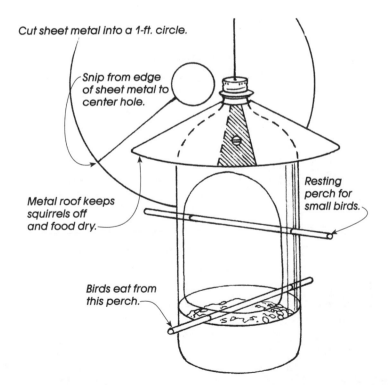

Cut sheet metal into a 1-ft. circle.

Snip from edge of sheet metal to center hole.

Metal roof keeps squirrels off and food dry.

Resting perch for small birds.

Birds eat from this perch.

Brightening the Indoors

Enjoying peonies indoors

Even if inadequate sunlight is keeping your peonies from blooming in the garden, you can still enjoy vases of these beautiful flowers indoors. Our peony bushes were already well established when we moved into our present home. As the years past, however, surrounding trees grew to shut out the full sunlight the peonies needed to bloom; they would bud, but not blossom.

Out of frustration one June, I cut a bunch of peony buds and greenery and put it in a vase on my desk. I had decided I'd just as soon look at buds as nothing, when, to my surprise, after two or three days the buds opened into full blooms.

I staggered the bud cutting and had peony flowers indoors for well over a month. The only real trick to this procedure is to pick the buds when they look as though they might open soon. Some buds never open, but even the buds themselves look nice in a vase.

–Leta Howes, Skowhegan, ME

Geranium flowers brighten the gray months

I like to enjoy the cheerful flowers of geraniums during the winter as well as during the summer. Plants that have been doing their best in the garden all summer, however, can be reluctant to continue flowering indoors all winter as well. I've found that by inducing a short period of rest in the fall, I can encourage plants to bloom freely again from winter until spring.

The rejuvenation process is simple. In early fall, I dig the geraniums out of the garden and prune both stems and roots back hard. I pot the plants in fresh soil in a pot they fit in snugly, but not tightly, and bring the plants indoors to a sunny window. I leave them alone for several weeks, watering them only as necessary. Then I give the plants liquid fertilizer at half strength at the next two waterings. (I don't fertilize much more than that because I find that my plants tend to produce leafy growth rather than flowers if I do.) By January or February, the geraniums should be back in bloom.

–Kathleen S. Van Horn, Rochester, NY

Workaday greenery

Spider plants satisfy my need for a bit of green at the office, where I work without windows, fresh air or natural light. Here's how I keep them healthy.

I start with a "baby," one of the countless daughters that spider plants produce at the end of trailing stems. I carefully detach the baby from its stem and float it in plain water until it produces roots. Then I transplant it to a container of potting mix and fertilizer, take it to the office, and set it under a fluorescent light from Friday morning to Monday morning. Three days of continuous light stimulate new growth. The plant now needs nothing more than water and a little fertilizer. If it ever looks peaked, put it under a fluorescent light again for a day or so. In an office that keeps the lights on all night, your plant may never need a boost.

–Dorene M. Pasekoff, Phoenixville, PA

Index

E

Earwigs, trapping, 103

F

Fertilizing:
    assembly-line method for, 61
    drip irrigation for, 78-79
Flats, making, 23-24
Fungicides, making, 108
Fungus gnats, controlling, 104

G

Gauge, watering, making, 80
Geraniums, growing indoors, 119
Germination:
    of hard-shelled seeds, 32
    petri dishes for, 34
    See also Seedlings, starting.
Gloves, as herbicide applicator, 106
Greenhouses, miniature, making, 21-23

H

Hoses, soaker, hold-down for, 81
Hostas, wildflower companions for, 68
Hot beds, making, 30, 39-40
Hyacinths, stem growth aid for, 50

I

Insects, controlling:
    on houseplants, 109-110
    lizards for, 109
    spiders for, 106

L

Leaves:
    dusting, 69
    shining, 69
    shredding, 3-4
Light boxes, making, 20-21, 24-25

M

Mildew, powdery, controlling, 107
Mulch:
    acorns for, 16
    applying, 14-15
    around trees, 12-13
    cheesecloth for, 17
    mixture for, 17

N

Newspaper, as barrier against pests and
    disease, 91

O

Overwintering:
    perlite for, 69
    polystyrene coolers for, 66-67

P

Peonies, bloom-forcing tip for, 118
Perennials:
    dividing, 46-47
    transplanting, 67
Plants, potted, preventing drying of, 73
Propagation:
    of African violets, 44-45
    of *Coreopsis rosea*, 45-46
    of pachysandra, 45

R

Rabbits, controlling:
    cat fur for, 91
    mesh bags for, 90-91
    shrubs for, 86
Raccoons, controlling, 88
Rainwater, catchers for, 70-73, 76-77
Reflectors, light, making, 18-19
Rodents, controlling:
    bone meal for, 85
    chicken wire for, 92
    daffodils for, 87
    dogs for, 92
    hot peppers for, 89
    pool hose for, 87-88
    traps for, 86
    See also Bulbs, protecting.
Roots, separating, 32
Roses:
    chopped banana skins for, 65
    borer deterrent for, 105
Row covers, uses for, 28-29

S

Seedlings:
    protecting, 38-39
    starting,
        corsage boxes for, 35-36
        egg shells for, 36
        measuring cups for, 33
        paper towels for, 37-38
        PVC pipe for, 35
        toilet paper rolls for, 37
    transporting, 31

Seeds:

Seeds:
    chilling, 30-31
    separating chaff from, 18, 29
    sowing, 43-44
Slugs, controlling:
    clay pots as traps for, 100
    eggshells for, 97
    pine needles for, 99
    shovels for, 99
Snails, controlling, 98
Soil, sterilizing, 31
Spider plants, growing indoors, 119

T

Tree branches:
    leaving snow on, 60
    spreading with clothespins, 60
    weights for, 63-64
Tulips:
    care of, 51
    planting, 54-55

W

Wasps, controlling, 99
Watering, deep, methods for, 74-76
Weeds:
    collecting, 111
    controlling,
        boiling water for, 102
        landscaping fabric for, 110
        large leaves for, 6
        newspaper for, 8-9
        walnut leaves for, 16
    pulling up, 111
Whiteflies, trapping, 104